FAITH, WHAT IS IT?

*Unlocking the code of the faith
of God and how to use it.*

PAUL PERESICH

ISBN 979-8-89130-643-1 (paperback)
ISBN 979-8-89130-644-8 (digital)

Christian Faith Publishing
832 Park Avenue
Meadville, PA 16335
www.christianfaithpublishing.com

All scripture references are from the King James Version of the Holy Bible unless otherwise noted.

Printed in the United States of America

CREATIVE POWER VERSUS CULTIVATING POWER

There is something very important that we must look
at before we start giving a definition to faith, God's
faith, which He has given us access to use.

God has limited creative power to Himself. He can speak words, and His words *instantly* come to pass. That is creative power. That's why when God speaks, things happen exactly as and when He says or has said.

In Genesis 1, we are given many examples of this during the creation of existence as we know it. The scripture in Genesis 1 says many times, "God said, and it was so." You can find God, the Father, doing this over and over throughout the whole Bible. Sometimes He is using cultivating power with His words instead of creative power. Because of this, some of the things He says take hundreds of years to come to pass. This is generally when He was dealing specifically with mankind and mankind's future.

Jesus Himself gave us examples of creative power using words. He spoke to a fig tree, and immediately His words affected the tree.

> *And Jesus answered and said unto it, No man eat fruit of thee hereafter forever. And his disciples heard it.* (Mark 11:14)

This is the record of Jesus speaking to the fig tree.

> *And in the morning, as they passed by, they saw the fig tree dried up from the roots. And Peter calling to remembrance saith unto him, Master, behold, the fig tree which thou cursedst is withered away.* (Mark 11:20–21)

His words had an immediate effect on the object that He focused them on, which in this situation was the fig tree.

He spoke to the wind and the waves, and immediately His words had an effect (Mark 4:39).

He spoke to sicknesses or diseases that were destroying people's physical bodies, and immediately the destruction caused by the sickness or disease reversed. They were made completely whole (Matthew 8:2–3).

This is creative power using words.

It is not the normal way that God allows the operation of man's words. He did not give us a constant direct connection to creative power, but He has it. Not only does He have it, but He also allows mankind to use and release cultivating power using words.

God has given us the ability to start the process of change through the release of our words.

What I am saying is a principle that Jesus taught over and over: we speak words, and our words take time to come to pass. I'll give you a few Scriptures on this.

A very familiar Scripture is Proverbs 18:21.

> *Death and life are in the power of the tongue and they that love it shall eat the fruit thereof.*

Notice this Scripture did not say, "They that love it shall eat what is instantly produced or created by the words that rolled off your tongue." No, it says you will "eat the fruit thereof."

Meaning, your words are going to start producing results, but just like fruit, it is produced over some time. It will take time to eventually reap a harvest from your words. It will take time for you to have what you say. I think the Lord did this so that we have time to undo the dangerous things that we can speak or release through words, which eventually in life can cause major problems or bring blessings. Jesus teaches this principle many times. His teachings reveal how the kingdom of God operates through man's life.

> *And he said, So is the kingdom of God, as if a man should cast seed into the ground; and should sleep, and rise night and day, and the seed should spring and grow up, he knoweth not how. For the earth bringeth forth fruit of herself; first the blade, then the ear, after that the full corn in the ear. But when the fruit is brought forth, immediately he putteth in the sickle, because the harvest is come.* (Mark 4:26–29)

Notice that the kingdom of God operates in the lives of men just like a farmer planting seed. It is a process that involves several factors that must take place before the seed produces the results that are desired. You could say that it produces the desires that were called for at the beginning of the cultivation process. I don't think I need to go through the explanation of how you need soil, water, and sunlight to bring forth a harvest, so I'm not.

Here is another scripture that should be very familiar to you that Jesus taught. In this teaching, He was specifically teaching the use of faith. What I want you to catch is the cultivation process. The cultivation process is started by the release of words for the purpose of bringing the desired result to pass. Jesus plainly shows it takes time.

We must recognize the fact that Jesus did not give us a teaching about man having the ability of creative power but man having the ability of cultivating power using words.

> *For verily I say unto you, That whosoever shall say unto this mountain, Be thou removed, and be thou cast into the sea; and shall not doubt in his heart, but shall believe that those things which he saith shall come to pass; he shall have whatsoever he saith.* (Mark 11:23)

Jesus did not say that the whosoever that is speaking to the mountain, immediately the mountain would be removed because of creative power through their words. No. What He did say is whosoever shall say unto the mountain (what that person said to the mountain) shall come to pass. Meaning there is a period before the harvest is reached before there is not a mountain in the person's life.

> That is cultivating power, which is what
> God empowered man with!
> Not creative power, which is what God
> himself is empowered with!

That right there should be enough to set you free from the pressure that we put on ourselves, or people put on us when we communicate things that are going on in our lives. We have things such as financial attacks, sickness attacks, things a family member is doing, or something that the devil keeps us in bondage to that we are striving to get out of. When we say something to someone about it, we are not putting ourselves under a curse, and we are not instantly creating problematic results.

I'll give you a quick example: say you're having a physical problem, and you go forward for prayer, or you ask someone to pray for you. They ask you what is wrong, and because of erroneous, superstitious teaching, you refuse to tell someone the physical problem you're having. You don't want to make a bad confession. For that person to know how to pray and what to pray against, it is necessary for you to tell them what is wrong. In saying the problem, it is not enhancing its ability to hurt you because you do not have creative power, you have cultivating power through your words.

Do you have a habit of continually confessing the problems in your life or repeating them over and over to everyone, even to the Lord, possibly trying to get His sympathy, impress people, or get people to feel sorry for you? Then you are continually planting your words as a farmer, and you will eventually reap a harvest of fulfillment of the seeds that you planted using words.

Yes, you should be considerate and thoughtful of the words you choose to speak because, *yes*, you're sowing seeds with your words. What I'm talking about, and what the Bible is talking about, is a lifestyle of word seed sowing. It causes a reaping or harvest of the lifestyle from your consistent choice of words.

That is how faith works weather for us or against us.

We are going to look at how God has set the whole process up. If we stay within the boundaries, or the rules and regulations of how He set it up for us to use, we will be successful in our use of faith and our bringing things to pass.

Faith is not just a religious term.

How it became known as a religious term could have only been through a lack of biblical understanding of the Scriptures. Many people link the word *faith* to their denomination or their belief system, which does not even come close to the Bible's definition of faith. I don't quite understand how this happened, especially in the church. The Bible rarely gives the idea that faith is a religious label or term to be used or assigned to a group of people or their denomination. What I mean is when you ask a person about their relationship with the Lord or where they go to church, many times they will say, "Well, I'm of the Baptist faith," or "I'm of the Pentecostal faith," or "I'm of the Catholic faith," when really to label those denominations as their faith is a misuse of the word faith.

Let me give you some scriptural examples which reveal this:

> *Through faith we understand that the worlds were framed by the word of God so that things which are seen were not made of things which do appear.* (Hebrews 11:3)

So if faith was a religious term, meant to be used to describe any denomination, the scripture would have to read: "Through my belief system," or "Through my Baptist, Pentecostal, Lutheran, or any other denomination, we understand that the worlds were framed by the word of God…"

Or…

> *But without faith it is impossible to please him: for he that cometh to God must believe that he is, and that he is a rewarder of them that diligently seek him.* (Hebrews 11:6)

If faith were a religious term, this verse would have to read: "But without my church denomination it is impossible to please God…" Or…

> *Who through faith subdued kingdoms, wrought righteousness, obtained promises, stopped the mouths of lions.* (Hebrews 11:33)

If faith were a religious term, this verse would have to read: "Who through their church denomination subdued kingdoms, wrought righteousness, obtained promises, and stopped the mouths of lions."

We can easily see through the Scriptures that mention the word or term faith that this is proven out. What we must do is erase this wrong understanding of faith from our thinking. We must renew our minds to God's definition of faith so we can learn how to use His faith with excellence to fulfill His will in our lives as instructed.

> *And be not conformed to this world but be transformed by the renewing of your mind that you may prove what is a good and acceptable and perfect will of God.* (Romans 12:2)

A very good scripture contained inside the Bible definitely shows the use of the word or the term faith being linked to an assembly or an organization. Even greater than that is being linked to or showing a way of life. Being a member of the body of Christ and adhering to biblical teaching is found in 1 Timothy 4:1.

> *Now the Spirit speaketh expressly, that in the latter times some shall depart from the faith.* (1 Timothy 4:1)

The statement the faith here is being used as an absolute (the faith), meaning the long-held, time-tested truths only found in the Bible. Truth that has sustained mankind this long, some will depart from. This is not speaking of a sudden departure from but a very slow departure.

What Paul is saying here is that the people who have claimed they are doing God's will have known what the Bible teaches. They have now begun to slowly depart from the teachings of the Bible and have begun accepting sin as a normal way of life: things such as drunkenness, sex outside of marriage, homosexuality, or lying. They begin the acceptance of a scriptural departure lifestyle, possibly because of their love for a family member or friend whom they don't want to hurt by telling them that the things they are doing are a violation of God's law. Jesus requires us, as opportunity opens, to speak the truth in love so they can ask Him for forgiveness with repentance. He is the only one who offered Himself so they can be forgiven.

Because of the choice to willfully sin, they cause themselves to be separated not only from God but also from those who choose to obey Him. If they leave their physical body while living in a lifestyle of sin, they will be separated from God forever. No matter what the cost, many must forsake family and friends (I did not say stop loving them). But because of their lifestyle, one must take a stance and be a light in the middle of a wicked and perverse generation.

A very good way to explain this is that mankind has had a path to follow, which the Bible shows to be the only successful way to live and conduct life. It is a path that, if you do not veer from, you will be blessed throughout your life, individual, family, or even nation. This doesn't mean you will not have conflicts, but that you will be blessed throughout your conflicts or troubles.

But if you veer from the teachings of the Bible, you are leaving the path of blessing that some of mankind has followed all these thousands of years. Some have chosen to depart from and not adhere to biblical teaching, yet they survive. Another way to express this is the statement "Some shall depart from the faith," which signifies that those who have walked in the light of God's word for many years and know how to live according to God's word and how to adhere to the long-held, time-tested teachings of the Bible which have illuminated their path of life will depart from the faith. This is a sure sign that we are in the last days. Now they have chosen to slowly step away from the light of God's word, believing and saying they are walking in a new light or on a new path, which leads them toward darkness and away from the light of God's word, thereby going off on a path that is not long held or time tested.

Anytime man or even nations tried to depart from the faith, they found out they couldn't sustain themselves, and whether an individual or a nation, eventually they failed miserably.

Only adherence to the word of God, the Bible, can sustain human life.

FAITH IS GOD'S IDEA

God is the one who authored faith; He is the one
who gave us examples of how to use faith, and He is
the one who helps us develop faith in our lives.

Looking unto Jesus the author and finisher
of our faith. (Hebrews 12:2)

So with those thoughts in mind, let's find out what faith really is. Let me share with you my testimony of how I started on this quest to know exactly what faith is. When I first received Jesus as my Lord and Savior, I knew something had happened on the inside of me the moment I prayed what Christians call the sinner's prayer. I didn't know what it was that changed inside me; I just knew there was a difference. I immediately started going to church and attending Sunday school by my own choice. My parents had raised me to be faithful in attending church, but around the age of sixteen, I stopped.

Now that I was attending church again, I started hearing God's word. During this same period in my life, a relative mailed me a cassette teaching on how to get my prayers answered. They did not know that I had received Jesus as my Lord. The reason they sent this cassette was to implant God's word inside me, believing for my salvation. A couple of the scriptures that were taught on this tape were from Matthew 21:22, where Jesus said,

> *If you have faith…all things that you shall ask in prayer believing you shall receive.*

Also in Mark 11:24, Jesus said,

> *Have faith in God…(or have the faith of God), what things soever you desire when you pray believe that you receive them and you shall have them.*

The whole purpose of the teaching was to get across the reality that when you call upon Jesus to forgive you of your sins and save you, He does so instantly. That happens by faith.

If you have this thing called faith, then when you pray, at that moment believe that you have received what you asked for, and it shall come to pass that you will receive it. I also learned that there is a period between when you say the prayer and when you receive the desired result. It could be a short while or it could be a very long time, but if you believe you received when you prayed, you will indeed receive because that's what the Bible says.

Except in salvation, other factors usually are involved between the time you prayed and believed and the time you received. If you will hold fast to what Jesus said concerning praying and believing, you will receive. He will see to it that His word comes to pass.

So from the moment you uttered the prayer, you begin to thank God for your answer. Praise and thanksgiving are what you do during the time you pray until the time you receive. This act is called standing in prayer, believing you receive. Thanksgiving should not be what you would because you received the answer to your prayer. Yes, you should definitely give praise and thanksgiving when you receive the fulfillment of your prayer. Praise and thanksgiving are what you do as a sacrifice during the whole time you are believing for the fulfillment of your prayer. This is what I have learned experienced believers call using their faith with purpose.

This set me in motion to start diligently seeking to find out what this thing called faith is, how do I get it, and how do I use it.

At this time in life, I needed a part for my car which was broken down, and I did not earn enough money to just buy the part. Everything I earned was barely enough to cover rent, food for two children, my wife, and myself—much less money for electricity and all the other things that go along with just surviving. So I acted on those scriptures, and I prayed for the money to buy the part, which actually cost around $93. At the end of my prayer, I said, "I believe I receive the money for the car part."

Really, what I did was decide that if I was going to believe for $93, I might as well go all the way and just believe for a $100 even, which to me felt like believing for a million. During this period, the person I worked for let me borrow the work truck. However, he charged me for using it and deducted the cost from my check before I even received my pay. How generous.

Every time I came home and saw my broken-down car in the driveway, instead of complaining, I would say, "Thank You, Father. I believe I receive the hundred dollars to fix my car," and I would quote the scriptures that I was using as the basis of my belief. I didn't realize that faith, God's faith, was being deposited in me every time I read those scriptures. And faith, God's faith, was being released each time I quoted those scriptures. Moreover, that faith, God's faith, was being activated or released every time I said, "Thank you. I believe I receive."

I don't recall exactly how much time went by, but it seems like two or three months. I stood in faith and believed that I received. Two couples came from Texas who did not know what I had prayed for or that I was standing in faith, believing I received the money. They also didn't know if I had received Jesus as my savior.

When they walked into my house, I was asked, "Do you believe God can speak to people?"

I said yes and told them briefly of my salvation story. The man who asked those simple questions reached into his pocket and said,

"God spoke to me at home in Texas and told me to bring you $100." He had a check that was already written out for that amount, glory to God. It wasn't hard to say at that moment, "I believe" and "I receive," and it wasn't hard to give praise or say "Thank You, Jesus," after I had in my hands the very thing I prayed for.

God's word which contains God's faith will work for you also if you will take the time to get His faith inside you. You must be willing to release His faith by speaking His word on purpose for a desired result, accompanied by thanksgiving.

There was another couple with this couple whom God had also spoken to about something for me. You see, I was asking the Lord for teachings about miracles, healing, and the infilling of the Holy Spirit with the experience of speaking in other tongues, which is just praying out of your spirit. This couple brought a briefcase with them. The other man said God spoke to him at home in Texas and said to bring me books and cassette tapes of teachings on miracles, healing, and the baptism in the Holy Spirit, which his briefcase was full of.

Do you think I was excited or what? It is safe to say that this beginning of seeing God's word be fulfilled in my life propelled me to be a person who never compromises God's word. Not even when other people, who call themselves believers but never act on God's word, never take a stand, and never see anything really come to pass label me as a fanatic.

For over forty years now, I have never backed down from acting on God's word and watching Him fulfill it over and over, even though sometimes it may take years. One thing I did find is that many times, my life has had to be completely changed or rearranged for my prayer to come to pass.

Remember, God works on a person's character to make them profitable to His kingdom. I am showing you what I learned over the years concerning real Bible faith, God's faith, what faith is, and how to use it.

Since I made the statement that faith is not just some religious word, let's find out what faith really is.

WHAT IS FAITH?

Faith is a power.

You may be able to better relate to faith as being spoken of as like an energy.

Like in the physical body, you really can't see the power or energy inside, but you can detect when you or someone else is full of energy. You can detect when you are low on energy. You can see its results when you properly use the power of energy. There are ways which energy is received, stored, and released.

You consume food which contains nutrients that are important for many different areas of your body. Your body naturally assimilates the nutrients and positions them where they will be most useful so that when you make a demand on the use of energy, which came from what you have eaten, your body has it readily accessible to be used through the power we call energy.

Much the same with faith, if we can learn these basic principles of how faith comes, how faith is stored or developed, and how faith is released, then we are on our way to becoming a great person of faith. You will have the ability to please God if you will just be willing to use or release your faith and put it to work.

Faith is a power or energy.

Faith is sort of like electricity. Electricity has been around since creation, and even a caveman could have used electricity had he known the laws that govern it. If we learn the laws that govern the power of faith, then we will be able to use them with excellence and accuracy anytime we desire.

Let's look at a verse in the way the King James Bible speaks of the verse without using the true Greek meanings of the words.

> *Through faith we understand that the worlds were framed by the word of God so that things which are seen we're not made of things which do appear.* (Hebrews 11:3 KJV)

God did not take a hammer, nails, a saw, and sawhorses and start building or framing the worlds. No, He had an image of what He wanted so He spoke (Genesis 1), and the result which He desired happened. The Bible records the power that was used to frame or assemble or cause the universe, as we know it, to come into being was a power called faith.

> *Through faith we understand the worlds were framed.* (Hebrews 11:3)

Now the true meaning of this verse: the definition of the Greek words used here, for the worlds, is not really talking in relation to creation, but meaning eras or ages or periods. Were framed means these eras or ages were changed by a man's use of this power called faith when he acted on what God had spoken to him. If you trace back in the Bible, each recorded instance of God speaking to a man a similar pattern was presented to each person. When acted on, faith was released and brought about the desired results.

They heard God's word, believed His word, then acted on God's word. These three principles can be used in any situation in life to bring to pass the desired results. Even you and I, if we hear God's word, believe God's word, speak His word or speak in line with His word, then act in line with His word, we will begin to see results.

For instance, Noah used faith, and because of this use of faith, he changed a whole age, from one era to another.

Hebrews 11 will give you example after example of this. Let's look at the very first time we have recorded God using faith, His faith.

In the beginning, when God spoke what He wanted to come to pass, the Holy Spirit used the power called faith which is contained inside God's word, and used it to create existence as we know it, just as is stated several times in Genesis 1.

> *And God said, Let there be light: and there was light.* (Genesis 1:3)

> *And God said, Let there be a firmament in the midst of the waters, and let it divide the waters from the waters.* (Genesis 1:6)

> *And God said, Let the waters under the heaven be gathered together unto one place, and let the dry land appear: and it was so.* (Genesis 1:9)

> *And God said, Let the earth bring forth grass, the herb yielding seed, and the fruit tree yielding fruit after his kind, whose seed is in itself, upon the earth: and it was so.* (Genesis 1:11)

> *And God said, Let there be lights in the firmament of the heaven to divide the day from the night; and let them be for signs, and for seasons, and for days, and years: and let them be for lights in the firmament of the heaven to give light upon the earth: and it was so.* (Genesis 1:14–15)

> *And God said, Let the waters bring forth abundantly the moving creature that hath life, and fowl that may fly above the earth in the open firmament of heaven.* (Genesis 1:20)

> *And God said, Let the earth bring forth the living creature after his kind, cattle, and creeping thing, and beast of the earth after his kind: and it was so.* (Genesis. 1:24)

In each of these recorded instances of God speaking, the result He desired, the power He released was called faith. Faith was contained inside the words that He spoke, and the Holy Spirit took that power, used it, and brought about the end result that God desired.

This power called faith is also what Jesus is using to keep everything in place and to sustain existence as we know it.

Hebrews 1:3 says speaking of Jesus, and upholding all things by the word of His power (or the power contained within His word).

The power that Jesus is using to uphold all things is the same power that He and God the Father used to create all things and the name of that power is called faith.

> *By the word of the Lord were the heavens made.* (Psalm 33:6)

And the power that is contained in His word and the power that was used to make the heavens is called faith. You and I can learn to use that same power since the power of faith is contained within His word. If we learn His word, this ensures His word is deposited within our heart, then inside our heart, faith is resident, and when we do the same as our heavenly Father and speak His word or speak in line with His word, then we release the same power He releases when He speaks His word, which is called faith. God's word coming out of God's mouth is God's word. God's word coming out of our mouth is still God's word.

I realize that we are not God, so when we speak, we do not usually get the instant results that He gets when He speaks. That is because He releases creative power. But we are His children and not merely His creation. If we have received Jesus as our Lord and Savior, and as we learn to imitate Him, we become better at producing results when we say what He says because we release cultivating power.

I think the reason Peter called the promises that God has spoken *"exceeding great and precious promises"* (2 Peter 1:4) is because these are God's words, and His words are greater than any earthly king. An earthly king's words are required to be fulfilled, just like an earthly king's decree or proclamation must come to pass. Even much stronger than a human king, the proclamation of the God and Creator of all existence must come to pass or be fulfilled.

That is why it is so important to know the promises or proclamations that are given for us to say and act on, releasing our faith on purpose for them to be fulfilled in our lives. Each of us should be continually increasing in our knowledge of God's word, or what the Bible says. We should know the location of where it is in the Bible and be able to find it and use it or share it with others.

I encourage you to learn God's word and to know it very well, so, at any given moment, you can say what God has said. You can speak into any situation or circumstance in your life or someone else's life and release the power contained within God's word to change your or their situation or circumstance, and that power is called faith.

Don't fool yourself and think that you're going to be able to say God's word once or twice and change your whole life or character. No, what you have done is start the process of change through the release of the power contained within God's word, and you will eventually start seeing results.

Jesus gave the greatest illustration of how to use this power called faith for the purpose of removing something out of your life in (Mark 11). He demonstrated on purpose the use of His personal faith on the fig tree.

> *And seeing a fig tree afar off having leaves, he*
> *came, if haply he might find any thing thereon: and*
> *when he came to it, he found nothing but leaves; for*
> *the time of figs was not yet. And Jesus answered and*

> *said unto it, No man eat fruit of thee hereafter for*
> *ever. And his disciples heard it.* (Mark 11:13–14)

I think Jesus was giggling when he was walking up to the fig tree knowing He was about to release the power of faith upon it for a personal demonstration of how to use faith. He was from that part of the world so he knew there would not be any figs yet. If you will notice, the Bible records that He made a decree, "No man eat fruit of the hereafter forever." He said this decree loud enough for those around Him to hear. Then he made the statement,

> Have faith in God, or have the faith of God.
> (Mark 11:22)

Meaning that it is necessary for you personally to have the God kind of faith. Then he said in verse 23,

> *Whosoever shall say unto this mountain, be*
> *thou removed and be thou cast into the sea and shall*
> *not doubt in his heart but shall believe that those*
> *things which he saith shall come to pass and you*
> *shall have whatsoever he saith.*

In His personal example, Jesus released the power of faith on the fig tree and then told us, when we want to remove something out of our life, to do like He did. Just release the power of faith, the God kind of faith, or the faith of God against the problems in our lives by speaking to them, and that power of faith which we released with our words will start the process to move the obstacle out of our life.

How can this happen?

Because faith is power, and if you and I learn what faith is and the process of how faith works, we will be on our way to being successful in our use of faith and in pleasing God by using faith.

But Jesus didn't just stop there. When He told us how to use the power of faith to push something out of our lives, He also said when we desire something to be in our lives, the way to receive it is with the power of faith. Jesus actually uses this very same principle for us, joining His faith to any prayer we pray when we believe we receive by Him making the statement, "Therefore I say unto to you," in Mark 11:24.

This is again Jesus releasing His faith for us. Because Jesus said, "I say unto you," while talking about the desires we pray for, He released His faith forever, so when we pray, His personal faith is also attached to ours to bring our prayer to pass. He said when we pray, we are to believe we have received what we asked in prayer, and the power or the force of faith will be in motion for the Holy Spirit to use, to get our desire to us, or to bring our prayer to pass in our lives.

Something very important you must never forget, within this verse of Mark 11:24, Jesus also said "shall come to pass." Meaning there is time involved. How much time? I don't know, and He didn't tell us. He just said when you pray believe that you receive and you shall have.

That's why the writer of the book of Hebrews was inspired to write Hebrews 10:35–38:

> *Cast not away therefore your confidence, which hath great recompence of reward. For ye have need of patience, that, after ye have done the will of God, ye might receive the promise. For yet a little while, and he that shall come will come, and will not tarry. Now the just shall live by faith: but if any man draw back, my soul shall have no pleasure in him.*

Once you release your faith, stay confident that heaven is working on bringing your prayer to pass. Knowing the Bible and the promises that God released for you is God's will. Once you pray, speak, and act in line with His word, then you need to let patience undergird and support you. The scripture says patience will help you receive the promise. A major part of receiving is up to you. Trust that Jesus is working.

> *For yet a little while, and he that shall come*
> *will come, and will not tarry.* (Hebrews 10:37)

When will you receive the answer to your prayer? I don't know. Until then, you just keep believing, keep thanksgiving active, and do not let your confidence go. This way of living was set in place by God, and He said this is how we are supposed to continually live.

> *Now the just shall live by faith.* (Hebrews
> 10:38)

He also says if we draw back, if we lose our confidence, if we do not let patience help, then He has no pleasure in us.

> *But if any man draws back, my soul shall have*
> *no pleasure in him.* (Hebrews 10:38)

Remember, without faith, it is impossible to please Him, but with faith, you have the possibility of pleasing Him. You just must be willing to use your faith and not cast away your confidence in God's ability to bring His word to pass.

Once you begin to use your faith on purpose, releasing the power of faith to move the mountains out of your life or to bring into your life the desires that you pray for, your life will never be the same. When you start seeing results because you acted on God's word by believing it and you released the power contained in His word by saying what He says, by speaking in line with the promises, it will become a lifestyle. However, you cannot let the devil defeat you in the arena of thought or feelings.

Could you imagine being the devil and seeing and hearing human beings release a power that they cannot see and they cannot feel, and they just do it out of obedience to what the Scriptures tell them to do, being led by the Holy Spirit? The devil sees these humans acting because of their loyalty to Jesus, their Savior, and because of their desire to please their heavenly Father. They basically, blindly obey what has been asked of them through the Scriptures. And the devil sees humans doing this, and the only way he can get them to not be successful with it is to deceive them to say something, believe something, or act in a repetitive way that disagrees or shows disobedience to the teachings inside the Bible, the promises inside the Bible, and the commands inside the Bible. Those who will stand their ground and hold on and just believe until they see their desire come to pass—there's nothing the devil can do to stop them.

I'll give you a scripture which shows this.

> *And what is the exceeding greatness of his power to us-ward who believe, according to the working of his mighty power, which he wrought in Christ, when he raised him from the dead, and set him at his own right hand in the heavenly places.* (Ephesians 1:19–20)

This power that is beyond great is the power of faith. That is what He raised Jesus from the dead with—faith —and that is what He raised us from the dead with—faith—his own personal faith.

> *And you hath he quickened* (old English word which means made alive) *who were dead in trespasses and sins; For by grace are ye saved through faith; and that not of yourselves: it is the gift of God.* (Ephesians 2:1–8)

Grace is God's willingness to do for you whatever it takes to change you from being dead in trespasses and sin to being spiritually alive. But faith is the power that He used to bring about the change, and He used His personal faith as a gift.

When you acted on the scriptures about salvation, there was nothing the devil could do to stop the effect of the release of the power contained inside God's word. At the same time, God deposits some of His personal faith inside you, for you to start using, for you to start developing and obtaining more faith so you can use this exceeding great and powerful thing called faith like He does, to change things.

FAITH IS A LAW

S imilar to the way gravity is a law.

When God set the law of gravity in motion, it has never ceased to be in operation or at work. Man cannot stop its operation; he can only figure out ways to override it. The only one who can stop gravity completely is the one who sets gravity in motion to begin with, and that is God.

The same with faith, since it is a law, then like the law of gravity and like God, when He set the law of gravity in motion, it cannot be stopped. So also you and I, if we take the effort to learn how to set the law of faith in motion and leave it in motion, it will produce results every time.

The devil has nothing he can use to stop the power of faith when a person releases it, except to get the one who released faith to stop it with their own words or actions.

You may understand this easier if I say, "Faith is a force."

We use the law or the force of lift to supersede the law or force of gravity to help an airplane fly. It is my understanding that if you cause more air to flow over the top of the wing of an airplane than the amount of air going underneath the wing, the law of lift starts to operate, and the plane rises off the ground and flies. It will keep flying as long as you keep the law of lift in motion. If you stop and do not keep the law of lift in motion, then the law of lift stops and the law of gravity starts to pull the airplane back down. We use the law or the force of faith to supersede the law of sin and death.

When Adam and Eve committed the original sin, they died spiritually, and the law of sin and death ruled, reigned, or was in force over all mankind. God had spoken to Adam that if he disobeyed Him, he would die.

> *And the Lord God commanded the man, saying, Of every tree of the garden thou mayest freely eat: but of the tree of the knowledge of good and evil, thou shalt not eat of it: for in the day that thou eatest thereof thou shalt surely die.* (Genesis 2.16–17)

The moment Eve ate the fruit of the tree of the knowledge of good and evil, she died. Then Eve gave to her husband to eat, and the moment Adam ate the fruit of the tree of the knowledge of good and evil, Adam died. They did not die physically because the Bible records Adam lived 930 years.

> *And all the days that Adam lived were nine hundred and thirty years: and he died.* (Physically) (Genesis 5:5)

Also, they did not die mentally or in their soul because they knew that a change had taken place and they feared and hid themselves. So how did they die? They died spiritually only and as a result of spiritual death, they eventually died physically. The law of sin and death was set in motion.

Up until this time, they did not have any children, so when they started having children, since everything reproduces after itself, all mankind was born spiritually dead. This is proven in the book of Romans.

> *Wherefore, as by one man (Adam) sin entered*
> *into the world, and death by sin; and so death passed*
> *upon all men.* (Romans 5:12)

This spiritual death had to be reversed, and the only way for that to happen is for somehow a man to be born spiritually again—from being spiritually dead to being spiritually alive.

Satan held the key of death over mankind since he led man to sin and die spiritually. So the only way to get man spiritually alive again would be for a spiritually alive man to go into the place of spiritual death and defeat the one who had the key to death. And the only way to get into the place of the spiritually dead is to become spiritually dead.

> *For this purpose the Son of God was mani-*
> *fested, that he might destroy the works of the devil.*
> (1 John 3:8)

Destroy the work which the devil accomplished through Adam and Eve, spiritual death, which has been passed to all mankind. Since Jesus has never sinned and Jesus is God's Son, also Jesus has always been spiritually alive, but He had to somehow be made spiritually dead. So He had to become a man, He had to be born of a woman like all mankind, but He could not have man's seed in Him; otherwise, He would have been born spiritually dead like all human beings.

So He had to be born of a virgin without man's seed causing the pregnancy in her. The seed that was placed inside the virgin's womb was the word of God. In fact, the Bible records the word of God being made flesh in the book of John.

> *And the Word was made flesh, and dwelt*
> *among us, (and we beheld his glory, the glory as of*
> *the only begotten of the Father,) full of grace and*
> *truth.* (John 1:14)

God the Father did not have to have sex with the Virgin Mary for her to become pregnant. No, but He did need to speak words that would contain His faith and then He would need to have the Virgin Mary accept or receive His word so that His word could become the seed inside Her womb to give birth to His son. I will show you this in the scripture where it took place.

The law of faith was released by the angel speaking God's word, and then all that was necessary was for the Virgin Mary to allow the law of faith to go to work in her life and produce the holy Son of God. Can you imagine being Mary the mother of God's Son?

We need to especially take notice that the devil could do nothing about it. Once the law of faith was set in motion, nothing could stop it except the one who set it in motion or the one to whom it was presented. That person had to choose to act upon the spoken word, and I am so thankful Mary said, "Be it unto me exactly as you said."

> *And the angel said unto her,* (The release of faith) *Fear not, Mary: for thou hast found favour with God. And, behold, thou shalt conceive in thy womb, and bring forth a son, and shalt call his name JESUS. He shall be great, and shall be called the Son of the Highest: and the Lord God shall give unto him the throne of his father David: and he shall reign over the house of Jacob for ever; and of his kingdom there shall be no end. Then said Mary unto the angel, How shall this be, seeing I know not a man? And the angel answered and said unto her, The Holy Ghost shall come upon thee, and the power of the Highest shall overshadow thee: therefore also that holy thing which shall be born of thee shall be called the Son of God. And behold, thy cousin Elisabeth, she hath also conceived a son in her old age: and this is the sixth month with her, who was called barren. For with God nothing shall be impossible. And Mary said,*

(The acceptance of God's word, the seed, containing God's faith)

Behold the handmaid of the Lord; be it unto me according to thy word. And the angel departed from her. (Luke 1:30–38)

And the Word was made flesh, and dwelt among us (John 1:14)

"The word became flesh and dwelt among us" is speaking of Jesus. Since Jesus didn't have man as His father, but God as His father, He did not have spiritual death inside of Him. He was the first man to ever be born spiritually alive, and He became God's second son, or as the Bible recalls His only begotten Son (Son by birth). God created Adam; he wasn't born, but God and Mary gave birth to Jesus; He was born or begotten.

So Jesus gave His life, being spiritually alive to become spiritually dead, so He could gain access into the place where those who are spiritually dead go when they leave their body at physical death and that place is called hell.

Jesus suffered spiritual death for three days, and then in that place of spiritual death, God spoke and said in Hebrews 1:5:

For unto which of the angels said he at any time, Thou art my Son, this day have I begotten thee? And again, I will be to him a Father, and he shall be to me a Son?

Jesus was the first person to be born from spiritual death to spiritual life, never to taste death again. He did all of this to take your and my place in spiritual death. If we accept what He did for us in taking our place, we will become spiritually alive; we will be born again spiritually.

The first spiritual birth was passed on to us through Adam. Since everything produces after its kind, and Adam was spiritually dead before having children, we were brought into the earth through our physical parents as eternal beings, all being born spiritually dead. The second spiritual birth only takes place as an act of choice to receive the sacrifice that God provided to bring a man out of spiritual death. God does not force this on anyone. He leaves this as an act of your will for you to make a choice to receive Jesus as your Lord, to receive His son who was sacrificed for your sin and for the sin of the whole world.

It doesn't matter whether you went to church all your life, or if you're a very so-called religious person; none of those matters. No religion can give you access to God,

> *Jesus saith unto him, I am the way, the truth, and the life: no man cometh unto the Father, but by me.* (John 14:6)

Only through the acceptance of Jesus giving His life for you do you get access to God the Father, and you miss going to the place where spiritually dead people go. You are then allowed to spend eternity with the spiritually alive, forever, in the place that is called heaven. If I were you, I would make the simple decision right now to say, "Thank You, Jesus, for what You did for me. I accept You as God's gift to me, and I receive You as my savior right now. Amen."

The Bible shows that this change from spiritual death to spiritual life takes place using faith contained inside God's word. The power or the law of faith is set in motion through speaking and acting upon God's words.

> For by grace are ye saved *through faith*; and that not of yourselves: it is the gift of God. (Ephesians 2:8)

Grace really means an impartation from God.

God imparts His life and nature to us when we receive Jesus as God's gift to us. At that moment, we become spiritually alive.

The power or the law that was used to get us birthed from spiritual death to spiritual life is the power or the law of faith. The Holy Spirit took that power that was released when we said, "Jesus, I receive You as my Lord."

At that moment, the Holy Spirit imparts to us the life and nature of God. He changes us from being spiritually dead to being spiritually alive, in an instant if not faster, by that power, by that law called faith.

When Adam died spiritually, he was no longer the son of God; he was merely God's creation because God's son Adam had died. But when Jesus took our place in spiritual death so that we could become spiritually alive, the moment we accept what He did for us, then once again we become sons of God or children of God.

> *But as many as received him, to them gave he*
> *power to become the sons of God, even to them that*
> *believe on his name.* (John 1:12)

People who don't read the Bible and don't listen to people teach the Bible correctly say dumb things like, "We're all God's children, but we're not." We are all God's creation. We become God's child when we become spiritually alive and the only way for that to take place is through the acceptance of the sacrifice that God Himself personally gave for you and me. That sacrifice has a name. His name is Jesus; He is also called the Lamb of God. He is called this because a lamb was used as a sacrifice for man's sin. John the Baptist even calls Jesus God's sacrificial lamb.

> *The next day John was back at his post with*
> *two disciples, who were watching. He looked up,*
> *saw Jesus walking nearby, and said, "Here he is,*
> *God's Passover Lamb."* (John 1:35–36 MSG)

God gave His only lamb, His son, as His personal sacrifice for man's sin. That's how much He loves you. So don't believe it when people tell you there must be other ways to get to heaven; there isn't.

There was only one spiritually alive man who was given as a sacrifice, and He doesn't have all these other false saviors' names. He has one name, and it is Jesus, and you would be wise to simply accept it like that and keep on going.

The moment you do this, you're going to notice such a change inside of you that you will realize you have been transformed from being spiritually dead to being spiritually alive; the difference will be noticeable. If you don't believe me, ask Jesus about it Himself. He is the only savior who can answer you.

You can pray to any and every so-called god or religious figure, and none of them, not one, will answer or help you because they are dead. They have passed into eternity with no ability to communicate. There is only one savior, and if you call on Him, He can and will answer and help.

His name is Jesus.

> *For the scripture saith, Whosoever believeth on him shall not be ashamed…*
> *For whosoever shall call upon the name of the Lord shall be saved…*
> Again, his name is Jesus. (Romans 10:11–13)

> But as many as received him, to them gave he power to become the sons of God, even to them that believe on his name:
> Even now, when you read these scriptures faith was deposited into your spirit.
> If you will choose to act on these scriptures by doing what they say you will be releasing faith, and the Holy Spirit will use your release of that power, that law, called faith and you will become what these scriptures say.
> You become a child of God, you get saved from eternal death. (John 1:12)

Romans 3:26–28 shows that it is the law of faith that was used to make us righteous (or again one with God).

> *To declare, I say, at this time his righteousness: that he might be just (righteous), and the justifier (the one who makes righteous), of him which believeth in Jesus. Where is boasting then? It is excluded. By what law? of works? Nay: but by the law of faith. Therefore we conclude that a man is justified by faith without the deeds of the law.* (Romans 3:26–28)

The moment you heard the words of the Bible and believed and spoke in line with the words that the Bible speaks concerning salvation, a law was set in motion—the law of faith, which caused you to overcome the law of sin and death. That law of sin and death governs the way the world lives, thinks, and acts. By using this power or law called faith, you overcome the world (the way the world thinks and acts), or you overcome spiritual death.

The Bible even says this in 1 John 5:4:

> *For whatsoever is born of God overcometh the world: and this is the victory that overcometh the world, even our faith.*

When you say, "Jesus, I receive You as my Lord and Savior," Jesus imparts into you His righteousness. Meaning if you so choose, you can think like God would have you think, you can speak like God would have you speak, and you can act like God would have you act. This would be the opposite of the way the world thinks or acts and would be in a manner which is pleasing to God.

All this happened through the release of the power or the law of faith. This is a principle that God the Father set in motion, and His whole kingdom operates on this principle, which was designed for our success. This principle of faith being a law is designed to be applied in every situation of life. You resist the devil with the word of

God, which is a release of faith. Then you stand your ground as the devil tests your faith, trying to get you to cast away your confidence in God's ability to fulfill His promises.

That is what Jesus did.

> *Then was Jesus led up of the Spirit into the wilderness to be tempted of the devil. And when he had fasted forty days and forty nights, he was afterward an hungred. And when the tempter came to him, he said, If thou be the Son of God, command that these stones be made bread. But he answered and said, It is written, Man shall not live by bread alone, but by every word that proceedeth out of the mouth of God. Then the devil taketh him up into the holy city, and setteth him on a pinnacle of the temple, and saith unto him, If thou be the Son of God, cast thyself down: for it is written, He shall give his angels charge concerning thee: and in their hands they shall bear thee up, lest at any time thou dash thy foot against a stone. Jesus said unto him, It is written again, Thou shalt not tempt the Lord thy God. Again, the devil taketh him up into an exceeding high mountain, and sheweth him all the kingdoms of the world, and the glory of them; and saith unto him, All these things will I give thee, if thou wilt fall down and worship me. Then saith Jesus unto him, Get thee hence, Satan: for it is written, Thou shalt worship the Lord thy God, and him only shalt thou serve. Then the devil leaveth him, and, behold, angels came and ministered unto him.* (Matthew 4:1–11)

If any form of sickness attacks you, resist the sickness with healing scriptures. Learn the healing scriptures, believe them, and speak them with expectations of total healing. The same with financial problems, family issues, or moral concerns. You take the time to find what God's word says about any area of life and keep God's word first place and final authority. Then act accordingly. Your situation will change.

FAITH IS A SUBSTANCE

I t's tangible, it can be applied to things. In Mark 11, Jesus applied faith to the fig tree with His words, and when His disciples asked Him concerning the fig tree, Jesus gave them the greatest teaching ever on faith when He made the statement "Have faith in God," in verse 22.

Some versions say, "Have the faith of God," or "Have the God kind of faith." Any way you say it, the meaning behind what Jesus said is that this is how you use the God kind of faith or how you use God's faith like God uses it.

You apply faith to things with words, whether it's a fig tree, a mountain, addiction, or poverty. You apply the substance of faith to anything, and you leave it there, and you let the power, the law, the substance of faith do its work.

How do you apply faith to things?

By speaking to the things you want to be changed. Once you release the power or energy of faith to something, once you set in motion the law or force of faith, once you apply the substance of faith to remove something from your life or to bring something into your life, even though you cannot see it—you generally also cannot feel that it is at work—it will produce results if you will only allow it to continue doing what you released it to do.

How do I do that?

By quoting the scriptures which address your need, that is where the faith came from. Make these scriptures first place and say them in the first person.

There is a major secret that somehow is not known by the church, and I have a real hard time understanding how the church misses it so big. Once you release faith, just leave it out there. Don't ever say anything opposite of the prayer you prayed for yourself or someone else. Stick with the command you made addressing what you want removed out of your life. *This is why declarations or decrees are so powerful.*

If they are spoken in line with God's word, then the Holy Spirit, the angels, and all of heaven can go to work bringing them to pass. Apply the substance of faith then let faith do its job.

I'll give you a testimony. My wife and I desired a house. So I found scriptures that speak of owning a house.

One of them was Deuteronomy 6:10–11:

> *And it shall be, when the Lord thy God shall have brought thee into the land which he sware unto thy fathers, to Abraham, to Isaac, and to Jacob, to give thee great and goodly cities, which thou buildedst not, and houses full of all good things, which thou filledst not, and wells digged, which thou diggedst not, vineyards and olive trees, which thou plantedst not; when thou shalt have eaten and be full…*

I grabbed ahold of that and some other scriptures concerning housing, and for six years I quoted, confessed, prayed, declared, and stood on them. During those six years, we looked at many houses and did not find a single one that would work for us financially or room-wise. I would not give up; I didn't let go of my confidence that God's word would fulfill itself. I believed I received a house that we could afford and would meet my family's needs.

Then one day, we were sent to look at a house. When we drove down the road and saw the house, we knew that was the one. We placed an offer and got it. During those six long years, the Lord was working on me to be able to purchase a house. You see we never owned anything before, so He opened the door for us to buy a trailer for $2,500. We paid it off for six years which allowed us to sell the trailer to afford the down payment of the house, a down payment which we would not have had if we hadn't bought the trailer.

Do not allow yourself to think that the Lord is not working for you and on you to fulfill His promises. He just needs you to trust in Him with all your heart and in all your ways acknowledge Him and He will direct your path.

FAITH IS A SERVANT

Like money is the servant of the one who possesses money, faith is the servant of the one who possesses faith.

Jesus gave us a teaching showing this in Luke 17:5–10.

> *And the apostles said unto the Lord, Increase our faith. And the Lord said, If ye had faith as a grain of mustard seed, ye might say unto this syca- mine tree, Be thou plucked up by the root, and be thou planted in the sea; and it should obey you. But which of you, having a servant plowing or feeding cattle, will say unto him by and by, when he is come from the field, Go and sit down to meat? And will not rather say unto him, Make ready wherewith I may sup, and gird thyself, and serve me, till I have eaten and drunken; and afterward thou shalt eat and drink? Doth he thank that servant because he did the things that were commanded him? I trow not. So likewise ye, when ye shall have done all those things which are commanded you, say, We are unprofitable servants: we have done that which was our duty to do.*

In this teaching, Jesus likens faith to a servant. The servant—faith—should be given assignments to accomplish. Each and every time something is accomplished by faith, we should turn right around and reassign our faith to accomplish something else for us because faith is a servant to the believer.

Jesus said, "If you have faith, you might say unto this tree," using the tree as an example. You might say to this unforgiveness, sickness, poverty, addiction, or attitude, even a low intelligence level. Then He told us exactly what to say to whatever it is you want removed from your life. "You be plucked up by your roots and you be planted in the sea." Then Jesus said, "And it should obey you." The thing you spoke to, yes, but even more so, the faith you released when you gave the command to do the work—it, the faith, should obey you.

Faith is your servant, just like you are Jesus's servant. He assigns us duties and expects us to carry them out completely. We assign our faith duties by the words we speak, and that pleases God. You may ask, "How do I assign faith duties to accomplish for me?" Through your prayers and through your declarations which are directly in line with the scriptures.

We should also use our confession of what God's word says about us purposefully, confessing His promises. Then simply believe your prayers will come to pass. Believe you will become the person the Bible says you are. Believe you will receive the fulfillment of the promises in the Bible for you. This is simple but not the easiest thing to do.

You have your fleshy feelings to override, as well as the constant thoughts from your soul—most of the time opposite thoughts than what the Bible says. Then you have the thoughts and feelings the devil gives you that you must override, not to mention the negative conversation other churchgoers or worldly people continually speak. No matter what anyone else says, you and I cannot let our servant faith sit idle.

When we bought the house I told you about in the last chapter, it was on a dirt road. During dry days, everything would be covered in dust: the car or truck, the inside of the house. Then on rainy days, the vehicle was covered in mud. On top of that, there was a sizable hill to climb, so we would slide all over the road trying to climb the hill to get out.

So I got my family together, pulled out my Bible, and looked up Matthew 21:22, which says:

> *All things that you shall ask in prayer believing*
> *you shall receive.*

Also in Mark 11:24, Jesus said,

> *What things soever you desire when you pray*
> *believe you receive them and you shall have them.*

I desired for that road to be paved. My wife and children had the same desire, so we were in agreement which made what we were about to pray even stronger.

> *Again I say unto you, That if two of you shall*
> *agree on earth as touching any thing that they shall*
> *ask, it shall be done for them of my Father which is*
> *in heaven.* (Matthew 18:19)

A paved road is a thing, so we qualified with what Jesus said about a desire. We also were on earth and in agreement, so we qualified for our Heavenly Father to bring it to pass. So my wife and I, our two young daughters, and, at that time, one toddler son walked up that road proclaiming the scriptures and declaring, "We say this road is paved." We did this many times over the next few months.

Something I need to share with you is that the road that we drove on to get to our road passed three other unpaved roads with families living on them. On our road, we were the only family. Common sense would dictate that if any roads out in our area were to be paved, they would be the ones with several families on them. Also, other than us living on our road was one house with two elderly people; the next nearest neighbors were a mile away in either direction. The mail lady would not even come to our house. We had to put our mailbox up one mile from our house. But each time we drove or walked that old country road, we would declare how nice it was to have our road paved.

One day when I came home from work, I noticed the road was graded really well. The next day, I noticed our road had little markers all down it. Then just a few days later, I came home, and our road was beautifully paved. Thank You, Jesus. Thank You, Jesus! My, my.

I always wondered what the county supervisors thought about when they decided to pave our road before the other roads with more families living on them. That day, I wrote in the back of my Bible: "On so-and-so date, by faith, Barber Road was paved."

God demands we have faith to please Him, but you must know how and be willing to use your faith if you are going to please God.

> *But without faith it is impossible to please him: for he that cometh to God must believe that he is, and that he is a rewarder of them that diligently seek him.* (Hebrews 11:6)

Since this verse states that without faith, it is impossible to please Him, then God is demanding that we have faith to have the possibility of pleasing Him. It also shows that just because you may be a possessor of faith does not mean you are automatically pleasing God. No, you must be able and willing to release, set in motion, apply, or direct the faith that you possess to please God.

Also, if God is going to demand that we have faith, His faith, then He is going to have to place faith in a position for us or anyone to easily receive it or obtain it, so it becomes our faith. We possess it, so we can choose to use faith at any time to please Him.

I thank God He has placed faith in an easily obtainable position for anyone to receive by hearing His words. Again, just because you possess faith does not mean you are pleasing God, but it does mean you now can please God if you choose to use your faith

> *Without faith it is impossible to please him.* (Hebrews 11:6)

But if we can become a possessor of faith, we now have the possibility of pleasing Him. The thing we have to do is learn how to obtain this power, this law, this substance, this servant called faith. Then be willing to use it to please Him.

I want to give you a few observations and references that the Scriptures make very plain about faith.

Faith can be developed, or faith can grow.

> *We are bound to thank God always for you, brethren, as it is meet, because that your faith groweth exceedingly.* (2 Thessalonians 1:3)

Faith can be weak, or faith can be strong.

> *And being not weak in faith, he (Abraham) considered not his own body now dead, when he was about an hundred years old, neither yet the deadness of Sara's womb: he staggered not at the promise of God through unbelief; but was strong in faith, giving glory to God.* (Romans 4:19–20)

You can be full of faith.

> *And Stephen, full of faith and power, did great wonders and miracles among the people.* (Acts 6:8)

Not everyone has faith.

> *Finally, brethren, pray for us, that the word of the Lord may have free course, and be glorified, even as it is with you: and that we may be delivered from unreasonable and wicked men: for all men have not faith.* (2 Thessalonians 3:1–2)

If you are willing to obtain, develop, and use your faith, then your faith will grow. We will be strong in faith, and we will be full of faith. When we do things by using our faith, believe me, it will be spoken of. For God to be just, God had to place faith in a position where it can be easily obtained by anyone.

How do we obtain the faith of God, or the God kind of faith?

FAITH COMES AND
IS OBTAINABLE

The Bible clearly tells us exactly how to receive faith or how to obtain faith.

*So then faith comes by hearing and hearing by
the word of God.* (Romans 10:17)

A proper definition of the scripture would be faith comes by hearing and hearing and hearing and hearing the word of God. Not faith comes by having heard the word of God. You need to keep a steady input of hearing God's word. Faith does not come by praying, or crying, or begging, or even speaking in tongues. No, the Bible is very plain on how faith comes.

*So then faith comes by hearing and hearing by
the word of God.* (Romans 10:17)

God's word is the vehicle He uses to transport or transfer His faith. So if you want to obtain faith to have the possibility of pleasing God, you simply put yourself in a position to hear God's word. Whether it's by reading the Bible, listening from your electronic devices, teaching CDs, or even being in a church that teaches the uncompromised truths of God's word from the Bible. Faith comes to you because faith comes by hearing and hearing the word of God.

Jesus gave a great teaching on this in Mark 4:9–20:

> *And he said unto them, He that hath ears to hear, let him hear. And when he was alone, they that were about him with the twelve asked of him the parable. And he said unto them, Unto you it is given to know the mystery of the kingdom of God (If I were you I would claim that!) but unto them that are without, all these things are done in parables: that seeing they may see, and not perceive; and hearing they may hear, and not understand; lest at any time they should be converted, and their sins should be forgiven them. And he said unto them, know ye not this parable? and how then will ye know all parables? The sower soweth the word and these are they by the wayside, where the word is sown; but when they have heard, Satan cometh immediately, and taketh away the word that was sown in their hearts. And these are they likewise which are sown on stony ground; who, when they have heard the word, immediately receive it with gladness; and have no root in themselves, and so endure but for a time: afterward, when affliction or persecution ariseth for the word's sake, immediately they are offended. And these are they which are sown among thorns, such as hear the word, and the cares of this world, and the deceitfulness of riches, and the lusts of other things entering in, choke the word, and it becometh unfruitful. And these are they which are sown on good ground, such as hear the word, and receive it, and bring forth fruit, some thirtyfold, some sixty, and some a hundred.*

Jesus Himself said that this is the way the whole kingdom of God operates. This is the pattern of God's standard operating procedures, and this is the pattern of how Satan operates to stop the word of God or the seed of God's word from producing results. All of it starts in mankind's heart, which is the soil or the reproductive or cultivating place for God's seed, God's word.

Jesus likens God's word to a seed which must be planted for the purpose of producing results. Let me say it like this: a seed is merely a vehicle or method of transportation for whatever it is that is contained inside the seed. Also, a seed does not care who is planting it. A seed just needs someone, a sower, who on purpose is willing to plant it to produce whatever is contained within the seed.

God created man so that man's heart or his spirit is the soil for His word, not his head. Satan also knows this. That's why whenever anyone hears God's word, he (Satan) tries to take away the word that was planted in man's heart. Satan wants to stop it from producing results in man's life. When God's word is heard, it immediately starts the process of working from within man's heart or spirit to begin the renewing or transforming of the mind to be willing to prove what is God's good, acceptable, or perfect will.

Satan has to take his best shot to stop that immediately.

In Mark 4:14–20, Jesus gave four examples of levels of desire and commitment to see God's word or the seed produce results while also showing the different strategies or distractions that Satan uses to remove or keep God's word from producing fruit from within man's heart or spirit.

> The sower is on purpose doing something in order to produce something.
> by the wayside people, these types of people hear God's word by accident, with no desire to hear it, no commitment, so no results. Easily taken from their heart by the devil.

Stony ground people, these types of people hear God's word with a desire to hear it, but
when problems arise because of God's word, they
exert no serious commitment, so God's word
is not allowed to even start to produce results.
Complete crop failure.

Stuck in a briar patch people, these types
of people have a desire to hear God's word and
a desire for commitment, but because of many
other commitments and giving their attention
to so many of the worlds attractions, they don't
allow the word time to fully produce so they get
upset at the Lord and say things like, "I tried the
Jesus thing and all it did was cause me more problems", so the word or seed produces no results.
All they really tried was the church thing. But, if
they're attending a church that does not teach the
uncompromised word of God and does not let
the Holy Spirit move among the people opening
their hearts to receive then there is no growth.
(Mark 4:14–19)

I can understand why they would give their attention to all
the worldly desires and attractions. Who would want to sit in some
church that's really a club week after week and not grow spiritually
at all? I would rather be doing something else. But if you get into
a church where God's word is being taught and the Holy Spirit is
touching the people and ministering to them, no entertainment in
the world can compare to the love of God, the grace of our Lord Jesus
Christ, and the communication of the Holy Spirit to His people.

Good soil people, these types of people have
a desire to hear God's word and are committed
to see results even though the problems or distractions of life come to them just like anyone
else. But because of their level of commitment,

and spiritual strength (heart strength), they allow
the word time to produce results and bear fruit.
(Mark 4:20)

It's like planting a garden. You can't expect to go out to the garden the next day and start eating the produce of what you planted. No, you know good and well that it's going to take some time before you harvest the product of the seeds you planted.

I'm telling you, if you give the word of God time in your life to really produce results, if you will stand through all the tests and trials that the devil will throw at you—trying to get you to change your mind, change your direction, and dig up your seed and throw it away—if you won't let that happen, then you are on your way to an adventurous life of faith.

I was in a restaurant with three other Bible-minded people. These people were more than just Christians; they were believers. We were talking about miracles that happened throughout the year, both in and outside of the church. Some of these miracles were very physically life-changing and amazing to the people who received them. We were also quoting scriptures that were used to release God's power, law, substance, and servant (faith) for the miraculous results. A man who was sitting in the booth next to us got up came and stood next to our booth and went on a furious rant about how we had ruined his meal. He claimed this was the worst time he'd ever had in a restaurant, having to listen to "all this religious garbage." He was upset that we would come into a public place and discuss "all this trash." (Give me a break.)

I share this because he literally fulfilled Mark 4:15. He was the person by the wayside where the word was sown. It went into his heart, even though he had no idea that he would be in a place that evening where he was going to hear God's word. Scriptures from the Bible, and immediately Satan started influencing him with reasons to berate us. This was to take the word out of his heart, which was sown accidentally by overhearing us talking in line with God's word while simultaneously quoting scripture.

Always remember, God's word is seed, and His seed carries within it His life and nature. You are His farmer or sower. So every chance you get, as you talk to others, slip in a scripture or at least speak in line with the Scriptures for planting to get results. The sower sows the word. A sower does something on purpose to get results.

Remember, faith comes by hearing.

> Faith comes by hearing and hearing by the word. (Romans 10:17)

Let me give some scriptural examples.

> *He therefore that ministereth to you the Spirit, and worketh miracles among you, doeth he it by the works of the law, or by the hearing of faith?* (Galatians 3:5)

If someone is yielding to the Holy Spirit's desire to manifest His gifts through them, is the Holy Spirit doing this because they have kept the law? They don't eat pork, they wash their hands before they eat every time, they don't lie, they observe all the feasts, they remember the Sabbath to keep it holy, they do the other things that are called the law, or they even act or dress very Jewish. Is that why the Holy Spirit has the opportunity to work through them and do miracles? No! He has the opportunity to work through them because they have heard the word of God, believed the word of God, and yielded to the Holy Spirit to fulfill the word of God to bless others or, as the scripture says, work miracles among you.

Remember, faith comes by hearing and hearing the word of God, but also faith is released by speaking and acting on the word of God. The Holy Spirit takes this release of faith when we speak the scriptures from the Bible that pertain to our need or request for someone else and does wonders with it. And the way that, as this scripture says, He that works miracles among you does it by the hearing of faith or the hearing of God's word and acting on God's word.

Remember, when you hear God's word, the Bible, faith is deposited in your heart every time. You then believe what you have heard, then you act on what you've heard, or even you just speak in line with what you've heard from the Bible. You are releasing faith, and the Holy Spirit takes that release of faith and starts the process of bringing to pass what God's word has said. That's why it is of utmost importance to know the Scriptures. If you don't know the Scriptures, then do as I did: call somebody who does know them and tell them you need them to give you a scripture for you to use in your prayer time.

Let's look at another example of faith coming by hearing.

> *And Cornelius told us how he had seen the angel standing in his house, saying, "Send word to Joppa and have Simon, who is also called Peter, brought here; he will bring a message to you by which you will be saved [and granted eternal life], you and all your household." (Acts 11:13–14 AMP)*

> And he shewed us how he had seen an angel in his house, which stood and said unto him, Send men to Joppa, and call for Simon, whose surname is Peter; who shall tell thee words, whereby thou and all thy house shall be saved. (Acts 11:13–14 KJV)

When Peter came and preached to Cornelius and those gathered with him concerning the Scriptures that were written in the prophets about Jesus and how they were fulfilled by God through Jesus's life, all those who heard the words that Peter spoke received faith for salvation, and instantly they believed what Peter spoke, and they were born again. How? By hearing words.

Remember what the angel said, "Who shall tell thee words, whereby thou and all thy house shall be saved."

This Scripture plainly shows us that men are saved by hearing words. Of course, they are because faith comes by hearing and hearing the word of God, and we are saved by grace through faith.

How about another example of faith coming by hearing God's word? This one is from the Old Testament.

> *And the angel of the Lord appeared unto him, and said unto him, The Lord is with thee, thou mighty man of valour. And Gideon said unto him, Oh my Lord, if the Lord be with us, why then is all this befallen us? and where be all his miracles which our fathers told us of, saying, Did not the Lord bring us up from Egypt? but now the Lord hath forsaken us, and delivered us into the hands of the Midianites. And the Lord looked upon him, and said, Go in this thy might.* (Judges 6:12–14)

The angel plainly told Gideon, "Your strength lies in your knowledge of God's word which you have heard through your Father's." So Gideon had faith because he heard the stories of the miracles which God had done. The angel was simply trying to get him to engage his faith by acting on his knowledge of God's word. This is also recorded in Hebrews 11:32–33:

> *And what shall I more say? for the time would fail me to tell of Gedeon, and of Barak, and of Samson, and of Jephthae; of David also, and Samuel, and of the prophets: who through faith subdued kingdoms, wrought righteousness, obtained promises, stopped the mouths of lions…*

What was the power, the law, the substance, or the servant that was used to accomplish these mighty works? Faith, God's faith, which comes by hearing God's word. If you have knowledge of God's word, therefore you are a mighty person of valor if you will just act on God's word.

When I first learned that faith comes from hearing God's word, I realized that I needed as much faith as I could possibly get. The next thing I realized was just because I possess faith does not mean I'm pleasing God. I will have to use my faith to please him. I then purposed myself to receive as much of God's word as I could so that I could possess as much of God's faith as I could contain.

At this time in life, our washing machine was broken; we only had one vehicle, two young children, also one in diapers. When I would come in from working anywhere from ten-to-fourteen-hour days, several times a week, I would have to load the dirty clothes up and take them to the laundromat. Before I would leave, I would place a cassette in the cassette tape player and tell my wife when I get to the laundromat. I would call her on the pay phone; this is way before mobile phones. When I called, I asked her to just lay the phone receiver on top of the cassette player and push play so I could hear the uncompromised teaching of God's word (from the Bible) while I was at the laundromat. I would stand there outside of the laundromat while the clothes were washing or drying, filling myself with God's word to fill myself with God's faith.

I have always tried to keep this level of desire and commitment to God's word working in my life. Why? Because Romans 10:17 says, "Faith comes by hearing and hearing by the word of God."

It took me a while, but I have the sense enough to realize that just like I ate food last week and that food produced energy for last week. But since the time that I ate last week until now, I have used all the energy that food produced. The same is true with you. You know what I have to do? I have to keep a steady input of good food into my body so that I have the physical energy to exert any and every time I need it.

Much is the same with faith. Just because I received God's word last week and faith came into me when I heard God's word—that was last week. I realize that sometimes I use up all the faith I have through the events and circumstances that happen in life. I have to keep a steady input of God's word into my spirit so that I have a steady flow of faith to be used to overcome all the things that come in life.

When you receive a phone call giving a bad report about one of your children or a relative, you use some of your faith to believe in them. When someone offends you, you use some of your faith to forgive them. When someone pulls out in front of you on the highway, you use some of your faith and hopefully pray that they get where they're going safely because they may be in an emergency, and that's why they're driving like they are, but you use some of your faith. When you are going through a tough financial situation, you use some of your faith to act and give some money while you believe for money to come to meet your needs. When you get a bad report from the doctor, you use some of your faith to believe in your healing. When you have a mountain needing to be moved out of your life, you use some of your faith to move it. When you see something that you would like to do or have, you use some of your faith to receive it.

All this faith that you are using needs to constantly be replaced and the way to replace it is with a steady input of God's word. So then faith comes by hearing, and hearing, and hearing God's word.

FAITH SPEAKS

If faith comes by hearing the word of God, then faith goes or is released by speaking God's word. Faith always says what the Bible says because the Bible is God's word. God's word is the vehicle He chose to transport His faith. If God releases His faith by speaking words, then we are going to have to release our faith by speaking words.

Throughout life, I've noticed that at first, it really feels strange to make myself think, speak, and act in line with God's word. It's because we have been programmed from childhood to think, speak, and act the way the world thinks, speaks, and acts. I found a key though: the more I practice this, the more natural it becomes. It is just like people who are rude or trash-mouthed. The more they practice being rude or vulgar, the more natural or common it is for them to be rude or vulgar to or in front of anyone. It just seems natural. You've probably noticed some people get really good at it.

The more you practice knowing God's word and speaking in line with His words while acting on His words, the better you get at it, and the more natural it becomes.

Remember in the book of Numbers when the twelve spies returned from searching out the land? The Bible records that ten of them brought forth an evil or wicked report. The words that they spoke contained no faith at all; therefore, God spoke of them as being evil or wicked in their speaking.

> *And they brought up an evil report of the land which they had searched unto the children of Israel, saying, The land, through which we have gone to search it, is a land that eateth up the inhabitants thereof; and all the people that we saw in it were men of a great stature.* (Numbers 13:32)

Can you imagine the nerve of these people? They ate manna for forty years, saw a pillar of fire at night and a cloud by day signifying God's presence, drank water from a rock, watched the Red Sea part and walked across on dry ground, witnessed Pharaoh's army drown, and observed all the plagues while partaking in none of them. Yet, they still walked completely by their feelings and sight. *You have* got to be kidding me.

They thought the way the world would think, and they spoke about their situation the way the world would speak about it. There was no trust or confidence in God whatsoever. They did not think as God would desire them to. They did not speak like God would desire them to speak; also they did not act like God would have them act. That is unrighteous.

Can you imagine the nerve of people who have grown up in church, seeing how the Lord has protected people, blessed people, and comforted people through all the things that life brings our way? Then for the sake of their children's friendships or more money or their business, possibly due to something sinful in these areas, they choose to reject the Lord's teachings and therefore reject church and probably anything to do with it. The Lord considers this to be you rejecting Him personally, and the root of this separation may be so that their disobedience doesn't hurt their conscience nearly as much.

My personal definition of righteousness is this: thinking as God would want you to think, speaking as God would want you to speak, and acting in a manner pleasing to Him.

I have friends and acquaintances. I allow some to get close to me and some I keep some distance from. Those close to me, I know that they're going to think, speak, and act in a way that I approve of. Then I have friends who we really aren't close because I know they're not going to think, speak, or act in a manner that I approve of. The first group of friends are righteous to me and the second group of friends are unrighteous to me. How much more so with the Lord and people.

Where do you find your relationship with Jesus?

The world, our own flesh, and the devil have tried to program us from childhood to be unrighteous. We were born spiritually dead, and because of that, we have no righteousness of our own or we have no ability of our own to think like God would have us think, speak like God would have us speak, and act like God would have us act. The only way for this to change is for a change to take place inside of us, in our spirit, and the only way for this to happen is through Jesus, by receiving Him and His righteousness. His ability to think the way God would have Him think, speak, and act. That is what is imparted into you and me at the point of salvation.

We find in the book of Isaiah the Lord is speaking to a certain group of people. He calls these people wicked and unrighteous, and He instructs them what to do.

> *Seek ye the Lord while he may be found, call ye upon him while he is near: let the wicked forsake his way, and the unrighteous man his thoughts: and let him return unto the Lord, and he will have mercy upon him; and to our God, for he will abundantly pardon. For my thoughts are not your thoughts, neither your ways my ways, saith the Lord. For as the heavens are higher than the earth, so are my ways higher than your ways, and my thoughts than your thoughts.* (Isaiah 55:6–9)

He is speaking to the unrighteous person, the person who has not received Jesus's righteousness. When you receive Jesus's righteousness, your ways and your thoughts start changing to be more like your heavenly Father's. You will find that the more you practice speaking in line with God's word, the better you will get at doing this. Speaking in line with God's word is good.

Remember the twelve spies? Ten of them spoke out of line with what God had said; God considered it an evil report (Numbers 13:32). Those spies died with all the people who believed the evil report. Joshua and Caleb were the only two who spoke in line with what God said; they lived, made it into the promised land, and were blessed.

If you're going to please God, you are going to have to be willing to release the faith you have received when you heard His word. You release it by speaking in line with His word.

Remember Romans 10:17:

> So then faith comes by hearing and hearing
> by the word of God.

Then it's easy to see that faith goes or is released by speaking the word of God. From the very beginning of the Bible, we have examples of this: God speaking His word, releasing His faith, and the Holy Spirit taking that release of faith and creating what God had said. See Genesis 1.

Then we have many examples of others who heard God speak or who were told what God had spoken to others. They acted on God's word out of trust and obedience to God, believing He would fulfill His word. We could say that all these people displayed an attitude of faith. This is a scripture that speaks to this.

> *We having the same spirit of faith, according as it is written, I believed, and therefore have I spoken; we also believe, and therefore speak.* (2 Corinthians 4:13)

This spirit of faith mentioned here is better understood as an attitude or camaraderie, such as in the military, or like being at a pep rally before the game to get everyone in the same mindset. You hear God's word; you believe God's word; therefore, you say God's word or you speak in line with God's word. That is the spirit or attitude of faith. That is why I can say faith speaks. I will give you a scripture about saying or speaking only in line with God's word, followed by several examples.

> *But the righteousness which is of faith speaketh on this wise, say not in thine heart, Who shall ascend into heaven? (that is, to bring Christ down from above) or, Who shall descend into the deep? (that is, to bring up Christ again from the dead) But what saith it? The word is nigh thee, even in thy mouth, and in thy heart: that is, the word of faith, which we preach.* (Romans 10:6–17)

Notice that this verse says that righteousness, which is of faith or became righteous *by faith*, speaks in this manner or speaks in a certain way. Let me give you an example: when you go to a fast-food restaurant to eat, you order by saying, "I would like a number four" or "number two." They know exactly what you want because you have spoken in the manner that the restaurant operates. However, if you went to a very nice five-star restaurant and you ordered, you would have to be very selective of each course of the meal that you were going to eat. So we could say you have to speak in a certain manner for the order to be placed. Just a little side note: you could dress in a way that shows you don't care how you look and order from a fast-food restaurant. But you may not get too far from dressing like that if you go into a five-star restaurant and order. Dressing nicely should at times represent our relationship with Jesus.

If there is a way those of us who have become righteous by faith must speak, then there is also a way those of us who became righteous by faith should not speak. That is what this verse is telling us, but for right now, let's just look at how we should speak.

> *But the righteousness, which is of faith speaks*
> *on this wise* (or in this manner). (Romans 10:6)

Verse 8 continues by saying,

> *But what does it say? The word is near you,*
> *even in your mouth and in your heart; that is, the*
> *word of faith, which we preach.* (Romans 10:8)

So when you hear God's word, whether by reading, listening to CDs, or sitting in a church and hearing the preaching, faith is going into your heart then your heart speaks out of your mouth what is in it. This verse is saying you and I are to choose to talk in line with what we know God's word says. When we hear God's word, His word goes into our hearts and is ready to come out of our mouths.

Let's look at this in the Bible.

> *Let us hold fast the profession of our faith*
> *without wavering (for he is faithful that promised).*
> (Hebrews 10:23)

Remember the four examples that Jesus gave us of desire and commitment to His word. That is similar to what this is talking about. The moment you start speaking in line with God's word, you are going to have to hold on to your release of faith by what you say. You must remember that the devil is going to try and get you to stop the working of your faith from producing results by getting you to change what you have said. He tries to pressure you to say something which is not in line with God's word.

> Let us hold fast the profession of our faith
> without wavering (for he is faithful that prom-
> ised). (Hebrews 10:23)

But don't do it; don't speak in a manner which you are not sup-posed to. Hold fast to your profession of faith. The seed you plant with your words will come to pass and produce results because faithful is He that made the promise. It just takes some time.

I really like what Galatians 6:7 says: "Be not deceived" (which actually means don't let anyone mislead you), "God is not mocked" (meaning this is a principal or a law that will not be altered or violated), and "Whatsoever a man sows that shall he also reap."

Remember Jesus gave the teaching that words are seeds in Mark 4, where He said the sower sows the word, and the seed is the word of God. So when you and I start speaking God's word on purpose to get results, God will not alter this law or violate it but will surely see to it that His word eventually comes to pass.

I have found what you and I must do is live a life of confessing the promises over ourselves knowing we are planting the seed of God's word. This verse actually means whatsoever a man sows and sows and sows that shall he also reap and reap and reap. A wise farmer regularly plants seeds all his life for a regular harvest in due season throughout his whole life.

> *Cast not away therefore your confidence, (your faith) which hath great recompence of reward. For ye have need of patience, that, after ye have done the will of God* (**the pattern**, learn the word, believe the word, say the word, act on the word) *ye might receive the promise. For yet a little while, and he that shall come will come, and will not tarry.* (God is going to see to it that His word will eventually be fulfilled) *Now the just shall live by faith: (living by His faith should be a lifestyle for us) but if any man draw back, my soul shall have no pleasure in him.* (Hebrews 10:35–38)

Don't give up, don't give in! Keep the pressure on by believing.

David knew very well that there was something to confessing God's word, along with holding on to God's word at all times. David knew that speaking in line with God's word was releasing some kind of power or some kind of law. That is why he so often confessed things by faith. Consider Psalm 23—the whole psalm is a faith confession.

> *The Lord is my shepherd; I shall not want.*
> *He maketh me to lie down in green pastures: he leadeth me beside the still waters.*
> *He restoreth my soul: he leadeth me in the paths of righteousness for his name's sake.*
> *Yea, though I walk through the valley of the shadow of death, I will fear no evil: for thou art with me; thy rod and thy staff they comfort me.*
> *Thou preparest a table before me in the presence of mine enemies: thou anointest my head with oil; my cup runneth over.*
> *Surely goodness and mercy shall follow me all the days of my life: and I will dwell in the house of the Lord for ever.* (Psalm 23:1–6)

Or look at Psalm 91, another confession of faith.

> *He that dwelleth in the secret place of the most High shall abide under the shadow of the Almighty.*
> *I will say of the Lord, He is my refuge and my fortress: my God; in him will I trust.*
> *Surely he shall deliver thee from the snare of the fowler, and from the noisome pestilence.*
> *He shall cover thee with his feathers, and under his wings shalt thou trust: his truth shall be thy shield and buckler.*
> *Thou shalt not be afraid for the terror by night; nor for the arrow that flieth by day; nor for the pestilence that walketh in darkness; nor for the destruction that wasteth at noonday.*
> *A thousand shall fall at thy side, and ten thousand at thy right hand; but it shall not come nigh*

thee. Only with thine eyes shalt thou behold and see the reward of the wicked.

Because thou hast made the Lord, which is my refuge, even the most High, thy habitation; there shall no evil befall thee, neither shall any plague come nigh thy dwelling.

For he shall give his angels charge over thee, to keep thee in all thy ways.

They shall bear thee up in their hands, lest thou dash thy foot against a stone.

Thou shalt tread upon the lion and adder: the young lion and the dragon shalt thou trample under feet. Because he hath set his love upon me, therefore will I deliver him:

I will set him on high, because he hath known my name.

He shall call upon me, and I will answer him:

I will be with him in trouble; I will deliver him, and honour him.

With long life will I satisfy him, and shew him my salvation. (Psalm 91:1–16)

Every verse is an engaging of faith. How about Jairus, in Mark 5:23, a ruler of a synagogue, seeking out Jesus because obviously he had heard or seen Jesus laying hands on sick people and them being healed? It could have been because Jesus ministered in His synagogue, so he released the faith he received when he sat in Jesus's meetings, and he heard Jesus teach and saw Jesus minister. He probably didn't even know he was releasing a power called faith, when he said to Jesus, "Come and lay Your hands on my daughter, that she may be healed, and she shall live." In other words, "Come. Do what You were doing in your meetings to my daughter."

That was a release of faith. Then in the same chapter, verse 27 states that the woman with the issue of blood, "Who when she had heard of Jesus, [faith came]" (verse 28). She said, "[Faith released] *if I may touch but his clothes, I shall be whole.*" And in verse 34, Jesus said to her, "*Your faith has made you whole,*" which is as much as saying, "When you heard of Me, you received faith." You said the end result of what you wanted and you acted, which was a release of your faith and your faith produced results.

Or how about, Matthew 8:2–3:

> *And behold, there came a leper and worshipped him, saying, Lord, if thou wilt, thou canst make me clean. And Jesus put forth his hand, and touched him, saying, I will; be thou clean. And immediately his leprosy was cleansed.*

The leper who came to Jesus must have heard that Jesus was laying hands on sick people, and they were being healed. He came to Jesus and said, "*Lord, if it be your will,* you can make me clean." (That was His release of faith which he received when he heard of how Jesus was healing people). Then Jesus Himself released His own faith, and Jesus touched the leper completing the desire and reason the leper came, *and said,* "I will be thou clean."

How about Matthew 8:5–10, 13?

> *And when Jesus was entered into Capernaum, there came unto him a centurion, beseeching him, and saying, Lord, my servant lieth at home sick of the palsy, grievously tormented. Jesus saith unto him, I will come and heal him. The centurion answered and said, Lord, I am not worthy that thou shouldest come under my roof: but speak the word only, and my servant shall be healed. And For I am a man under authority, having soldiers under me: and I say to this man, Go, and he goeth; and to another, Come, and he cometh; and to my servant, Do this, and he doeth it. When Jesus heard it, he marvelled, and said to them that followed, Verily I say unto you, I have not found so great faith, no, not in Israel… And Jesus said unto the centurion, Go thy way; and*

as thou hast believed, so be it done unto thee. And his servant was healed in the selfsame hour.

Jesus could have said to him, "As you have said, so be it unto you or to your servant." The centurion said what he believed. Jesus Himself said in Matthew 8:5–13, "The greatest faith of all is faith that speaks." We are talking about the centurion saying to Jesus, "Just speak the word only, and my servant shall be healed." The centurion acknowledged that Jesus's words were His servants, and Jesus acknowledged that His servants, which are words, carry a power within them called faith.

My personal favorite example of faith is in the Old Testament, found in the book of Joshua, chapter 6.

> *Now Jericho was straitly shut up because of the children of Israel: none went out, and none came in.*
>
> *And the Lord said unto Joshua (God releasing His faith)*
>
> *See, I have given into thine hand Jericho, and the king thereof, and the mighty men of valour.*
>
> *And ye shall compass the city, all ye men of war, and go round about the city once. Thus shalt thou do six days.*
>
> *And seven priests shall bear before the ark seven trumpets of rams' horns: and the seventh day ye shall compass the city seven times, and the priests shall blow with the trumpets.*
>
> *And it shall come to pass, that when they make a long blast with the ram's horn, and when ye hear the sound of the trumpet, all the people shall shout with a great shout; and the wall of the city shall fall down flat, and the people shall ascend up every man straight before him…*
>
> *And Joshua had commanded the people, saying (Joshua releasing faith),*

> *Ye shall not shout, nor make any noise with your voice, neither shall any word proceed out of your mouth, until the day I bid you shout; then shall ye shout.*
>
> *And it came to pass at the seventh time, when the priests blew with the trumpets, Joshua said unto the people, Shout; for the Lord hath given you the city.*
>
> *So the people shouted when the priests blew with the trumpets: and it came to pass, when the people heard the sound of the trumpet, and the people shouted with a great shout, that the wall fell down flat, so that the people went up into the city, every man straight before him, and they took the city.* (Joshua 6:1–5, 10, 16, 20)

If you look at Joshua 1:8, you will see that God told Joshua to meditate in His word day and night. Why? Because God knew Joshua would need to release a tremendous amount of faith continually for the rest of His life to bring Israel into the fullness of the blessing of the promised land. God knew faith comes by hearing and hearing by His word (this actually means by hearing it over and over again, not by hearing it one time or by having heard it but by a continual repeat hearing). So He told Joshua to meditate on His word day and night.

Joshua also knew that he would have to focus this power that is contained inside God's word on the walls of Jericho and the way to do that would be by only saying exactly what God said, or speaking in line with what God said. That is why Joshua commanded the people, "For the next seven days, do not make a sound!"

> *And Joshua had commanded the people, saying, Ye shall not shout, nor make any noise with your voice, neither shall any word proceed out of your mouth, until the day I bid you shout; then shall ye shout.* (Joshua 6:10)

He personally was committed, and he made the people also be committed to saying only exactly what God had told them to say, how God told them to say it, and when God told them to say it—no complaining, no gripping, no gossip, not even a whisper of spreading doubt!

Joshua received God's faith by hearing God's words or God's instructions on how Israel was going to defeat Jericho. Then Joshua released God's faith by speaking God's words or speaking in line with God's word when he gave the instructions he had received from God to the people of Israel. So Joshua received God's faith when he heard God's words, then Joshua turned around and released God's faith and imparted God's faith into Israel when he told them the words that God had told him; therefore it is recorded in the book of Hebrews.

> *By faith the walls of Jericho fell down, after they were compassed about seven days.* (Hebrews 11:30)

This must become a lifestyle; we must learn to live by faith. So if you see yourself lacking faith, know that you may not be lacking faith but you may just be short on your knowledge of God's word. Because faith comes by hearing and hearing by the word of God, and if faith comes by hearing, then faith is released by speaking.

I found very early in my personal life that I must be like Joshua and read and meditate on God's word day and night to keep a steady input of God's word into me, which produces God's faith. This steady input keeps my faith at a proper level, so I have faith available to release at any given moment. Doing this for nearly forty years has made my way prosperous and given me good success.

I must remind you how important it is to the Lord that we have this understanding or comprehension of faith. It's so important that He made the statement, "Without faith it is impossible to please him" (Hebrews 11:6). Paul, led by the Holy Ghost, prays in this way for the church.

> *For this cause we also, since the day we heard it, do not cease to pray for you, and to desire that ye might be filled with the knowledge of his will in all wisdom and spiritual understanding; that ye might walk worthy of the Lord unto all pleasing, being fruitful in every good work, and increasing in the knowledge of God.* (Colossians 1:9–10 KJV)

Also four different times in the Bible, this statement is made: "The just shall live by faith." This receiving and releasing of faith must be as natural to us as a fish swimming or a bird flying. Simply put, this should be a natural reaction to everything that happens or comes our way in life. We release faith, we engage faith, and we activate our faith.

Then keep your mouth shut so you do not withdraw your faith from what you released it upon. I have at times told myself and other people, "What you need to do is get a hold of some duct tape, and tape your mouth shut once you have prayed the prayer of faith or once you have released your faith to remove something out of your life." If you cover your mouth with duct tape, then at least you can't say anything opposite to what you believe.

FAITH SEES

If I know how to get faith, then I'm on my way. Now I just have to learn how to use it.

I have heard Brother Kenneth Hagin say, "If I know how to get money, I'm on my way. I just need to learn how to properly use it to be successful." Many people have money, but they do not know how to handle it or use it. Therefore, their money does not make them successful. It is the same with faith. If you have heard God's word, then you have faith. Many people don't know how to use faith, so therefore their faith does not produce results for them, even though they have everything they need for success.

Sometimes, people have what I call faith accidents. Someone hears the Bible's promises, and then they quote them and say they believe in them, and it comes to pass. They do not even understand how it happened. Maybe someone needs prayer for something, and they request someone to pray for them. The person praying uses a scripture or scriptures in their prayer, and they receive the answer to their prayer without even realizing the faith working behind it that gave the Lord the door of opportunity to bring it to pass. This was the release of faith, which came by hearing God's word.

This is a very poor way of communicating this, but to mark your thinking, I'm going to say it like this: You must be able to use your imagination and see yourself possessing what you desire to receive it, or the desired change in your life, before it ever happens in the natural physical realm.

I don't know if you could ever catch me saying, "I'm just waiting for the manifestation." This is because I believed I received the manifestation the moment I prayed or the moment I was prayed for by someone. From then on, I either never talk about my situation to anyone, or I continually give thanks and keep an inner image of what I will be like when it does happen naturally. If I do ask for a prayer, it generally is for prayer that my faith does not fail, and I stay strong and endure. As far as I'm concerned, it has already happened the moment I prayed or was prayed for.

Eventually, my situation or need will change to where it can be seen. From my view, it's already changed, or inside me, I see it already. Since I see it, if I'm going to talk about it, I'm going to talk and act as if it is already done.

While we look not at the things which are seen,
but at the things which are not seen: for the things
which are seen are temporal; but the things which
are not seen are eternal. (2 Corinthians 4:18)

The things which you see with your physical eyes are subject to change. And 2 Corinthians 5:7, "For we walk by faith, not by sight." I will show you Jesus using this very principle, or lifestyle, in His own personal life.

Then he took unto him the twelve, and said
unto them (faith released, faith speaks), *Behold,*
we go up to Jerusalem, and all things that are writ-
ten by the prophets concerning the Son of man shall
be accomplished. (Luke 18:31–33)

This shows where Jesus received the faith when He heard or read all the things that were written by the prophets concerning

Himself. That is when faith came to him. How? Through hearing God's word, faith comes.

> *For he shall be delivered unto the Gentiles,*
> *and shall be mocked, and spitefully entreated, and*
> *spitted on: and they shall scourge him, and put him*
> *to death: and the third day he shall rise again.*

Jesus is seeing Himself suffer, die, be buried, then rise again. Remember, things that He is seeing with His physical eyes are subject to change. He is walking by faith that He will accomplish what is necessary to obtain salvation for us. As horrible as it may be, He is believing in it. Again, Jesus used faith.

> *Let not your heart be troubled: ye believe in*
> *God, believe also in me. In my Father's house are*
> *many mansions: if it were not so, I would have told*
> *you. I go to prepare a place for you. And if I go*
> *and prepare a place for you, I will come again, and*
> *receive you unto myself; that where I am, there ye*
> *may be also. And whither I go ye know, and the way*
> *ye know.* (John 14:1–4)

Faith sees. Jesus is very selective with His words because He only speaks what the Father tells Him to speak. He knows anything the Father says will be filled with His Father's faith, so Jesus is releasing God's faith for our future on purpose.

Jesus is saying, "I am looking toward," or "I am seeing," or we could say He is looking forward to what He is seeing in His spirit. With the eyes of His spirit, He is seeing Himself going and preparing a place for us. He is seeing Himself one day coming back to receive us to Himself and bringing us to the place which He prepared for us. He is looking with the eyes of His spirit. He is seeing by faith.

When I was a young Christian and first learned these principles, I realized there were some things in my life that needed to change, or let's say they needed to be removed from my life. One of them was smoking cigarettes and marijuana.

Since I was learning God's word and knew that faith was coming into me because of Romans 10:17—"Faith comes by hearing and hearing by the word of God"—I knew that I would have to release this faith that was inside of me to free me from smoking. One of the Scriptures I held onto was Romans 10:10, which says, "For with the heart man believes unto righteousness and with the mouth confession is made onto salvation."

My inner image was me inside a jail cell, being held in bondage by smoking. And as the scripture said, "With the mouth, confession is made unto salvation." So to me, salvation would be me leaving the jail cell held hostage by cigarettes and marijuana and being free from them. My inner image was me free from smoking, and my confession was, "I am no longer in bondage to smoking anything."

I held onto that confession for two years and spoke it over and over and over. I also held onto my inner image of not being a person who smokes. Thanks be to God; I eventually became the person on the outside that I was on the inside. I believed I was free from smoking the moment I believed and started my confession, releasing my faith through my words, which brought to pass the reality of those scriptures which I had an inner image for years.

If you're going to have success using your faith, you are going to have to learn how to do this. In the natural, it seems wrong, but in the Lord's realm, it is the way to change things. If you want things to change in your life, the best thing to do is learn to do it His way as fast as you can.

In Psalm 27:13, David put it this way:

I had fainted, unless I had believed to see the
goodness of the Lord in the land of the living.

FAITH STANDS

If there's one thing I have found over the years, it is that the devil eventually wears out. If you can stand your ground, hold fast to your confession, don't sway in your believing, and endure. You will outlast the devil, and your victory will surely come.

Paul in Ephesians 6 called faith a shield. In fact, he said, "Above all, above everything else." In other words, he was saying, "Make sure if you do anything, you do this—get a good hold of that shield of faith and stand with a solid, firm grip believing."

Sometimes, when you are standing, confessing the scriptures, and believing for them to come to pass, you see Satan shooting fiery dart after fiery dart at you. You look over at the front of your shield, and there are red-hot fiery darts stuck in there; your shield is glowing red. You don't think you can stand there and hold your shield up for another moment. But you just hold on! Your faith will eventually quench all of them, and Satan will run out of effort. He will run out of fiery darts to attack you with, and you will be victorious!

Remember the principle that Jesus gave us in Mark 4. It speaks of the sower who sows the word. Anytime the word is sown, Satan comes immediately to take away the word which was sown. The same principle applies to you and me when we sow God's word into situations or desires in our personal lives through prayer, declarations, and confession. Satan comes immediately to try and stop us from allowing the word to bring the desired result.

Surely you don't think the devil is going to let you and me just use our faith freely, bringing to pass our desires without any resistance. We would crush his kingdom immediately. That is why he fights so hard to keep our understanding in the physical realm or the arena of the five senses. He does not want us to learn how to operate heavenly principles and heavenly rules of operation, which we are to use for the purpose of making his kingdom submit and yield to the cultivating power of releasing and engaging our faith.

> *And when ye stand praying.* (Mark 11:25)

> *And Jesus answering saith unto them, Have faith in God* (or this is how you use the God kind of faith). *For verily I say unto you, That whosoever shall say* (the release or activation of faith) *unto this mountain, Be thou removed, and be thou cast into the sea; and shall not doubt in his heart* (what you are doubting in your heart eventually comes out of your mouth), *but shall believe that those things which he saith shall come to pass* (there is time involved, how much time, however long it takes for your faith to bring it to pass, that's how much time)*; he shall have whatsoever he saith. Therefore, I say unto you, What things soever ye desire, when ye pray, believe that ye receive them, and ye shall have them. And when ye stand praying.* (Mark 11:22–25)

Jesus is teaching that once you have spoken to your mountain, or you have prayed and asked for your desire, there is a time of standing involved. This means you cannot sway; you cannot be moved; you cannot depart from what you have said nor from what you have believed you receive.

That is the real meaning of faith—being unmoving, unflinching, uncompromising, unwilling to bend, unwilling to break, and never giving up, no matter how hard it gets or how heavy you seem to be weighed down. You keep holding onto and believing the word of God. Believing it will come to pass. That is the meaning of faith. That is what Jesus meant when He said, "When you stand praying." In other words, once you have spoken to your mountain or you prayed for something you desired, you stay in that prayer mode until your desire comes to pass. I'll give you a few examples, but first, let me show you something else in Jesus's teaching here that is very important.

> *And when ye stand praying, forgive, if ye have ought against any: that your Father also which is in heaven may forgive you your trespasses. But if ye do not forgive, neither will your Father which is in heaven forgive your trespasses.* (Mark 11:25–26)

Unforgiveness overrides the use of your faith and causes it to become deactivated, disengaged, or inoperative. After all, it is God's faith that you are using, and He says, if you do not forgive, He will not forgive you your trespasses. Your use of the God kind of faith gets put on hold. Think about it for a second—He was willing to forgive you while you were spiritually dead and while you were a sinner. How much more is He expecting you to do what He did? You have to forgive others who trespass against you.

> *And be ye kind one to another, tenderhearted, forgiving one another, even as God for Christ's sake hath forgiven you.* (Ephesians 4:32)

> *For if, when we were enemies, we were reconciled to God by the death of his Son, much more, being reconciled, we shall be saved by his life.* (Romans 5:10)

God, the Father, did not hold back anything when He used His faith to save us through the death of His Son. Likewise, He is expecting us to not hold back anything in following Him in forgiveness by using our faith to forgive, just as He did us. Faith is, and should be, your trigger mechanism for everything in life to stay in line with the word of God and the fulfillment of His promises coming to pass in your life—your knowledge of His word, your belief of His word, your saying what His word says, and your acting on what His word tells you to do. This is the pattern established in the Bible by God Himself, and that is how all the elders obtained the good report and accomplished what is written of them in Hebrews chapter 11.

> *So then Faith comes by hearing and hearing and hearing the word of God* (a continual input to sustain a continual output of the God kind of faith). (Romans 10:17)

When you receive a phone call giving a bad report about one of your children or a relative, you use some of your faith to believe for them. You may pray something like this, "Father, in Jesus's name, You know where my child or my relative is, and You know what they're doing. You are the only one who has an answer to bring them out of it or through it. I release them to You, and I ask You to do whatever it takes to keep them alive and turn them to be in Your perfect will. Send people to them to minister Your word to them and set them free. In Jesus's name."

When someone offends you, you use some of your faith to forgive them. You pray something like, "Father, that person really hurt me by what they did. The pain that I feel really makes me angry, but because You have told me to forgive, I forgive them, and I let it go."

When you are going through a tough financial situation, you use some of your faith to believe for money, so you go give some of the money that you have, even if it's a tiny amount. You do it on purpose to act in faith to fulfill the Scripture: "Give and it shall be given to you." You remind the Lord of Himself to ask you to do that, and He will start the process of bringing you out of your financial bind.

You get a bad report from the doctor, so you use some of your faith to believe for your healing first and, if need be, that the doctors do not make any mistakes. You may have a mountain needing to be moved out of your life; use some of your faith to move it. When you speak to it (whether it's poverty or anger or fear), you speak to it and say, "Get out of my life, be removed, and be cast into the sea." You believe that those things which you have said will come to pass. Believe that you shall have whatsoever you say because you have spoken to your mountain; therefore, it will remove. That is using some of your faith. You may see something that you would like to do or have; use some of your faith to receive it.

All of this faith that you are using needs to
constantly be replaced, and the way to replace
it is with a steady input of God's word.

Not only are you using your faith in each of these situations, but you are also usually in a constant standing of faith mode for good results in each of these situations. Standing in faith is continually putting a demand on your faith level. Like when you work hard, you're putting a constant demand on your energy level, and your energy must be replenished. If you don't, you will slowly grow weak. You won't even notice how weak you are getting until you are at the point of being not worth anything much physically.

The devil realizes that if he can keep a constant drain on your faith and keep your attention off of replenishing and keeping your spirit strong, then you will eventually get to the place where your spirit is so weak and your faith level so low that you won't be at the place you were a day or two ago, or a week or two ago, or a month or two ago. If you don't watch it, you'll fall to the place you were a year or two ago. Standing in faith is not for the fainthearted; it is for the ones determined to be successful at all costs.

My wife could not have any more children because she was Rh negative. They said if she became pregnant, she could possibly lose her own life and the life of the child, or they both could die. She was pregnant with our third.

She had bled almost the whole nine months during the second pregnancy and was told to stay in bed the whole time, but she never did. She carried on like normal, and everything came out okay. But before the third pregnancy, we had accepted Jesus as our savior. The moment she said, "I think I'm pregnant," I grabbed my Bible and pulled out some of the scriptures that speak of "what things soever you desire," which we have already covered, and some other scriptures that talked about the Lord taking care of those with their young, and He will not shut the womb. We also named the baby and believed we received a boy.

This was the day she came home, and the doctor said, "You're pregnant." No one knew except us and the Lord. Ultrasound was just beginning to be developed, but we chose not to even do an ultrasound. We chose to go totally by faith and believe we receive a healthy child, a healthy mother, and a successful delivery.

For the next seven months, anytime someone said, "I heard your wife is pregnant," I would say, "Yes, she is, with a boy," and give them the child's name. Most people thought I was nuts, and most Christians would sort of roll their eyes and say, "You can't believe for something like that."

Then my comment sometimes would be, "You can't believe for something like that, but I can."

Seven months later, she gave birth to a healthy baby boy, and everything the doctor said usually happens to Rh-negative mothers didn't happen. When our son came out, he was crying; I said his name, and he instantly stopped crying. We even went on to have another son. Thank You, Jesus.

My reason for telling you this is that for seven months—seven long months—I felt the spiritual pressure of "How dare you try and believe you receive a son? How can you force your wife to go through this knowing what the doctors have already said?"

The spiritual pressure that was placed upon me came from worldly church people. I would talk to them about the stance we were taking, and they would make their stupid comments like, "You've been watching those TV preachers," and other comments like that. It was crushing. I didn't even have a single Christian channel on my

TV. When you only received five or six channels back then, there certainly weren't any that would be considered a Christian channel.

On top of that, there was persecution from within the church, from Christians who really weren't believers but were faithful church members. They were trying to talk me out of believing instead of joining with me and saying, "I agree, brother. So be it." Do you know what I had to do for those seven long months? Having done all to stand, I had to stand! And I did stand and have the son to prove it.

I've made the statement before that sometimes, when you release or activate your faith for your desire to come to pass, God may have to rearrange your whole life, so you are in a position to be able to receive what you asked for in prayer.

You can believe beyond your faith level, and you will never receive it because it's beyond your ability or your faith's ability to bring it to pass. Some people believe for $1 million, and they go their whole life believing in it but never receive it. Why? Because what it would take for the Lord to make you ready to handle $1 million might be more than what you're willing to go through. It might take more time, require more effort, may need to be more disciplined or demand more correction from you. Therefore, the effort it takes to get you to the place where you can have or handle $1 million never happens because you personally were not able to get to the place for it to come to pass.

I'll give you an example: We live on the Mississippi Gulf Coast, only a few miles from the Gulf of Mexico. When my children were young, I saw no reason why we shouldn't have a boat. I mean, we live right here at the edge of the United States. Everyone has a boat here, but we didn't because we couldn't afford one.

I knew the way to get one was to know what the Bible says about getting your desires met. I must believe what the Bible says, declare what the Bible says, and then start acting as if the Bible is going to fulfill itself, and I'll have the desired result. So I prayed using Matthew 21:22 and Mark 11:24 and believed I received a boat. I actually went by dealerships, looked at boats, picked the one I wanted, and believed in it.

Now at the time I did this, we had three children and were driving an early-model, compact Toyota Corolla. The whole family would pack in like sardines, and that was our mode of transportation. When I believed I received a boat, I hadn't considered that I had no means of towing a boat. I could barely afford the gas for the Toyota to commute to work each week. We struggled to afford groceries and the necessities for all three kids. Yet I prayed and believed I received a boat.

As the years went by, I continually thanked the Lord for that boat. About ten years later, I was working on someone's house. Parked underneath their shed was the exact boat I had prayed, believed, and was standing for ten years ago. I asked him what he was going to do with his boat, and he said he was going to sell it. When he told me the price, I knew that I already had that much money saved up, but—I want you to catch this—in those ten years, my income had grown enough to where I was able to buy a used truck and used car. (Side note: I have never purchased anything on credit. I have paid cash for everything except a trailer and a house.)

Now I was able to afford the gas that it took to go back and forth to work and take care of my family and the vehicles. We could afford our groceries and some of the other needs for raising kids. What I want you to catch is that ten years before, I couldn't have had that boat because I would not have had any way to tow it home or to the water. I could not afford gas for the vehicle we were driving, much less the boat and all the other things it takes to own a boat. But the Lord had rearranged my life completely to where I was capable of owning a boat.

It was all in place, and when I finally saw the boat I had prayed for for almost ten years, I was able to afford it and buy it. We used the exact boat many, many times. I stood for ten years believing I received the exact boat I had prayed for. For ten years, every time I thought of that boat, I gave thanks to the Lord for the boat that my family and I enjoyed. For ten years, I didn't ask again for the boat; I just rejoiced in the fulfillment of the word of God without ever having seen the fulfillment of it in the natural, but in my heart I had it, and my mouth reflected what was in my heart. I did not doubt it.

I was not moved. I stood firm that I have that boat, and I thank the Lord for it; it is mine. I have it now, and if I have ought against any, I forgive. I keep my heart clean. Thank You, Jesus.

Question: Did you catch the testimony I just gave you?

My life is full of testimonies like that, testimonies of over and over again praying for things for myself, praying for miracles for others, believing for others' healing and deliverance, and standing in faith and standing in faith and standing in faith, watching some come to pass quickly and watching some come to pass after many years.

The secret is faith stands.

Standing in faith is not the easiest thing to do, but it is doable and during your time of standing the Lord will strengthen you, if you only believe. God established this principle, and it is the same in each area of His kingdom. This is His standard operating procedure for you, for me, or for anyone. Learn His word, believe His word, say what His word says, and act on what His word says. That is a kingdom principal that will never be changed and is a requirement for us to arrange our lives.

When you start learning God's word, faith comes to you and is deposited in your heart. The question is will you release that faith or activate that faith by acting on what you have learned or heard out of God's word?

For instance, when I learned,

> *And he said unto them, Go ye into all the world, and preach the gospel to every creature. He that believeth and is baptized shall be saved; but he that believeth not shall be damned. And these signs shall follow them that believe; In my name shall they cast out devils; they shall speak with new tongues; they shall take up serpents; and if they drink any deadly thing, it shall not hurt them; they shall lay hands on the sick, and they shall recover. So*

> *then after the Lord had spoken unto them, he was received up into heaven, and sat on the right hand of God. And they went forth, and preached everywhere, the Lord working with them, and confirming the word with signs following. Amen.* (Mark 16:15–20)

When I first heard and learned this Scripture, I didn't know how to preach the gospel nor how to talk to anyone about Jesus. Besides that, I was scared stiff to try. But the Scripture told me to do it, so I had to begin talking to people, telling them what Jesus had done in my life and what He wanted to do in theirs. Every time I did that, I was activating and releasing my faith, and the Lord was at work, helping me become better and better at it. He helped me because I was pleasing Him, using my faith, acting on His word which told me to preach the gospel to every creature.

That's when I also saw the other signs that accompany a believer, and I wanted to be more than just a churchgoer. I wanted to be a believer, or a doer of the word, not a hearer only. I started practicing acting on each of those signs that Jesus said would follow or accompany those who believe. But one of them seemed to be another area where fear would keep me from acting—that was laying my hands on the sick for them to recover.

What I had to do was quote and quote these scriptures over and over. Every time I did, faith was being deposited in my heart. My faith level was rising, and then finally the day came when someone spoke of having some form of sickness, whether it was a cold, a disease, or cancer. My faith level was at a proper level to give me enough courage to ask if I could lay my hands on them for Jesus to heal them. By being willing to do what Jesus expected of all believers, I stumbled across something that was amazing to me.

The easiest people you can help get to receive their healing through the laying on of hands are those who have very little or no knowledge at all about the Bible. The ones who are not attenders of church. The ones who had knowledge of the Bible and who were faithful to a local church—it really didn't matter which denomination—I found it very hard to get any of them to receive Jesus's healing power through the laying on of hands.

That is when I realized those who know God's word, the Lord expected them to believe His word, say His word, and act on His word to get their own personal results. They are not to be depending on someone else to do all the work for them. It is like when they come up for prayer; they're coming up for a treatment, and the person who was laying hands on them and praying for them is supposed to be doing all the work. I found that God, the Father, expects His children to grow up and mature in their own use of faith.

If I find my courage level dropping, and my desire to act on God's word dropping, then I know I must replenish my spirit with God's word. His word deposits inside me God's personal faith, which He requires me to use to please Him. The same goes for you. You have to examine yourself regularly and check your spiritual strength level. If you don't do this, probably no one else will.

I am amazed that in the body of Christ, there is no personal evaluation. Really, not even any corporate evaluation of its members. Everyone seems to get away with their own personal free-for-all. The way they think it should be, the way they believe, the way they say the Lord is leading. They believe that everything they do is being directed by the Holy Spirit without ever asking the question of themselves or definitely not asking anyone else, if they personally could be out of line, or could I have done this better, could it have been my emotions or my flesh running wild. Then blaming what I did and their wrong decisions on the Lord.

> *Examine yourselves, whether ye be in the faith;*
> *prove your own selves. Know ye not your own selves,*
> *how that Jesus Christ is in you, except ye be repro-*
> *bates?* (2 Corinthians 13:5)

In my personal life, I've had a lot of reproving, rebuking, and exhorting by the Scriptures first, which is what the Lord uses for correction, and then by ministers who are willing to speak the truth in love and not make me be a duplicate of themselves. They allowed me to have my own personality and character with the Lord developing that. God's principle or God's pattern was at work in me without me even realizing it. The pattern: know God's word, believe God's word, say what God's word says, then act on what God's word says to act on.

I have used the same pattern in all facets of life. I gave my way out of debt. I have taken unto myself the sword of the spirit and beat the devil back many, many times in many circumstances of life. I have used the word of God over and over, which He sent to heal me. I have heard His word, believed His word, and spoke His word over my marriage, my children, my job, and many other areas of my life. The Lord will do the same for you.

The word of God and the faith that comes from hearing God's word must be the trigger mechanism that is released in every situation of life. The importance you place on your level of faith must be really important to the Lord for Him to say, "Without faith, it is impossible to please Him" (Hebrews 11:6).

To you and me, our knowledge and understanding of what faith is, how it comes, how to develop it, and how to use it properly should be of utmost importance. It should be right there with learning how to walk in the love of God. You can do this; set your heart to learn God's word—yes, by going to church, but not only by going to church, by reading His word yourself, by listening to teaching. There are so many avenues and ways to hear God's word taught, preached, and ministered through the technology that is available today.

Then believe God's word. Believe it to the place where you're willing to talk about it no matter what others think. Make God's word first place in your life and talk about it as if it is the first place in your life, whether anybody else believes it or not. You believe it, then put your belief in action, activate your faith, release your faith, and speak to things in your life and things in others' lives, expecting God's word to move and change your situation or their situation. Be a doer of the word, not just a hearer. When you have done everything you have to do, then stand. If you find yourself in a place where you feel like what you're doing isn't working, then you need to know more. You ask the Holy Spirit to fill you with the knowledge of His will in all wisdom and spiritual understanding.

The Holy Ghost through Paul gave us a prayer to use,

> *Wherefore I also, after I heard of your faith in the Lord Jesus, and love unto all the saints, cease not to give thanks for you, making mention of you in my prayers; that the God of our Lord Jesus Christ, the Father of glory, may give unto you the spirit of wisdom and revelation in the knowledge of him: the eyes of your understanding being enlightened; that ye may know what is the hope of his calling, and what the riches of the glory of his inheritance in the saints, and what is the exceeding greatness of his power to us-ward who believe. (His faith) according to the working of his mighty power, which he wrought in Christ, when he raised him from the dead, and set him at his own right hand in the heavenly places.* (Ephesians 1:15–20)

FAITH GIVES PRAISE
AND THANKSGIVING
FAITH WORSHIPS ON PURPOSE

I am amazed that most people think praise thanksgiving or worship is what you do after you get what you have believed for. That is so far from the truth. If faith is the bullet that is released at the target, then praise thanksgiving and worship are the gunpowder behind the bullet that propels it for the desired results.

> *And it came to pass, as we went to prayer, a certain damsel possessed with a spirit of divination met us, which brought her masters much gain by soothsaying: the same followed Paul and us, and cried, saying, These men are the servants of the most high God, which shew unto us the way of salvation. And this did she many days. But Paul, being grieved, turned and said to the spirit, I command thee in the name of Jesus Christ to come out of her. And he came out the same hour. And when her masters saw that the hope of their gains was gone, they caught Paul and Silas, and drew them into the marketplace unto the rulers, and brought them*

to the magistrates, saying, These men, being Jews, do exceedingly trouble our city, and teach customs, which are not lawful for us to receive, neither to observe, being Romans. And the multitude rose up together against them: and the magistrates rent off their clothes, and commanded to beat them. And when they had laid many stripes upon them, they cast them into prison, charging the jailor to keep them safely: who, having received such a charge, thrust them into the inner prison, and made their feet fast in the stocks. And suddenly there was a great earthquake, so that the foundations of the prison were shaken: and immediately all the doors were opened, and every one's bands were loosed. And at midnight Paul and Silas prayed, and sang praises unto God: and the prisoners heard them. And the keeper of the prison awaking out of his sleep, and seeing the prison doors open, he drew out his sword, and would have killed himself, supposing that the prisoners had been fled. But Paul cried with a loud voice, saying, Do thyself no harm: for we are all here. Then he called for a light, and sprang in, and came trembling, and fell down before Paul and Silas, and brought them out, and said, Sirs, what must I do to be saved? And they said, Believe on the Lord Jesus Christ, and thou shalt be saved, and thy house. and brought them out, And he took them the same hour of the night, and washed their stripes; and was baptized, he and all his, straightway. And they spake unto him the word of the Lord, and to all that were in his house. And when he had brought them into his house, he set meat before them, and rejoiced, believing in God with all his house. And when it was day, the magistrates sent the serjeants, saying, Let those men go. And the keeper of the prison told this saying to Paul, The magistrates have sent to let you go: now therefore depart, and go in peace. But Paul said unto them, They have beaten us openly uncondemned, being Romans, and have cast us into prison; and now do they thrust us out privily? nay verily; but let them come themselves and fetch us out. And the serjeants told these words unto the magistrates: and they feared, when they heard that they were Romans. And they came and besought them, and brought them out, and desired them to depart out of the city. And they went out of the prison, and entered into the house of Lydia: and when they had seen the brethren, they comforted them, and departed. (Acts 16:16–40)

Paul and Silas did not allow themselves to be spiritually weak, carnally minded, or flesh-dominated. They didn't cry out to God saying, "Why, Lord, why are you doing this?" No, they didn't even let any of that cross their lips. Neither should you and I, even when we are in the hardest place and the biggest test of our lives. That's why the testimony of Paul and Silas was written, to show us how to act and talk during our greatest trials.

Praise and thanksgiving are a major part of a mature Christians life. Really it should be a major part of a Christian baby's life if they are being taught correctly. Praise and thanksgiving should be a foundational teaching of how to make the faith you released or activated successfully for how to defeat the devil.

There are testimonies throughout the Bible of how confused the devil gets when people start worshiping, praising, and thanking the Lord before they ever even get the victory or can even see the victory, especially when everything looks like it's going to be absolutely total failure, like there's no way out and there are way too many obstacles, and it is impossible to get success. Praise, thanksgiving, and worship probably really burn the devil up and really make him so hot that we would have the nerve to offer the sacrifice of praise right in the middle of our hardest time. At the same time, it thrills our heavenly father and is absolute positive proof to Him that we have learned His word, and we believe and trust in His word. We are willing to confess His word and act on it even in the face of what looks like defeat.

> *By him therefore let us offer the sacrifice of praise to God continually, that is, the fruit of our lips giving thanks to his name.* (Hebrews 13:15)

A sacrifice costs you something.

That's why it's called a sacrifice—you must give something up. In your time of testing and trial, to offer praise, thanksgiving, and worship, you have to give up your pride.

You have to give up your emotions. You have to give up your desire to look good in front of people and most of all you have to give up your desire to want to point your finger at God and be mad at Him for not rescuing you. The truth is, He has already done everything and set you up for success if you and I will just learn, believe, confess, and act on His word.

Praise and thanksgiving are not only a requirement, but these are an attachment to our prayers. Whether we are speaking to a mountain to get something out of our life or whether we are asking for something to come into our life.

> *Be careful for nothing; but in everything by prayer and supplication with thanksgiving let your requests be made known unto God.* (Philippians 4:6)

This is also a requirement in all situations in life to keep the peace of God dominating you, spirit, soul, and body.

> *And the peace of God, which passeth all understanding, shall keep your hearts and minds through Christ Jesus.* (Philippians 4:7)

Can you imagine being the devil, hearing you praising and worshiping Jesus in everything, every situation, every test, every trial, every victory, every time you pray, every time you go anywhere, every time you do anything, you offer praise, you give thanksgiving, and you worship the Lord Jesus? That must absolutely drive him nuts.

We should not wait to offer praise and thanksgiving to God after everything is settled down and is just as we like it. No, we do this right in the middle of every situation. Establish your heart to take time and thank Him every day. Thank Him when you wake up. Thank Him when you are getting ready for your day. Thank Him during the day and throughout the day, thank Him during your study time, and thank Him when you lay your head down at night, and He gives rest for your body, peace for your soul, and comfort for your spirit.

I only know of one thing that will propel your faith, undergird your faith, and keep your faith in the place of being able to see the victory, while being able to call things which be not as though they were and keep your faith at a proper level so that it overcomes the world. Time spent in thoughts filled with the instructions to you. The stories told and the promises in the Bible. The only other thing that I know that does this is praying with the help of the Holy Ghost, praying in the spirit.

When you feel the devil trying to loosen the grip of your faith on the mountain that you have applied your faith to, by your words, don't retreat! Strengthen your faith and maintain your confession. Remind yourself and him that your faith is at work, and it will accomplish the task that you released it to do.

Remind your mountain that you have applied your faith to it and, as far as you're concerned, it has moved out of your life. Your path is clear, your victory is here, and when you're through doing that, start to praise and shout the victory. Give thanks to the Lord again and again and again. God likes to strengthen you during your use of faith, as you are speaking His word, while you are standing your ground. Jesus gave us an excellent example of this.

> *And there came a voice from heaven, saying,*
> *Thou art my beloved Son, in whom I am well*
> *pleased. And immediately the Spirit driveth him*

into the wilderness. And he was there in the wilderness forty days, tempted of Satan; and was with the wild beasts; and the angels ministered unto him. (Mark 1:11–13)

And Jesus being full of the Holy Ghost returned from Jordan, and was led by the Spirit into the wilderness, being forty days tempted of the devil. And in those days he did eat nothing: and when they were ended, he afterward hungered. And the devil said unto him, If thou be the Son of God, command this stone that it be made bread. And Jesus answered him, saying, It is written, That man shall not live by bread alone, but by every word of God. And the devil, taking him up into an high mountain, shewed unto him all the kingdoms of the world in a moment of time. And the devil said unto him, All this power will I give thee, and the glory of them: for that is delivered unto me; and to whomsoever I will I give it. If thou therefore wilt worship me, all shall be thine. And Jesus answered and said unto him, Get thee behind me, Satan: for it is written, Thou shalt worship the Lord thy God, and him only shalt thou serve. And he brought him to Jerusalem, and set him on a pinnacle of the temple, and said unto him, If thou be the Son of God, cast thyself down from hence: for it is written, He shall give his angels charge over thee, to keep thee: and in their hands they shall bear thee up, lest at any time thou dash thy foot against a stone. And Jesus answering said unto him, It is said, Thou shalt not tempt the Lord thy God. And when the devil had ended all the temptation, he departed from him for a season. And Jesus returned in the power of the Spirit into Galilee: and there went out a fame of him through all the region round about. (Luke 4:1–14)

This is a perfect picture of Jesus using the pattern God has established for all of us. He knew the word of God, He believed the word of God, He spoke the word of God, and He acted accordingly. That is the way He defeated the devil (but there is something you must catch here). Doing this He released His faith, and He needed to be restrengthened spiritually and the Lord God His father made sure He was. The Bible gives a record of this in Luke saying He returned in the power or the strength of the spirit. Mark gives a record of this saying, and the angels ministered unto Him.

USING FAITH IS WORK

From the very first record we have of faith being used, it is recorded that it was spiritual work. There was spiritual action involved; it involved spiritual labor, even for God the father Himself.

> *Thus the heavens and the earth were finished, and all the host of them. And on the seventh day God ended his work which he had made; and he rested on the seventh day from all his work which he had made.* (Genesis 2:1, 2)

I wish I could say this faith thing was easy, but it's not. If it was easy, then everybody would be in on it. But since it takes spiritual work and a lot of spiritual effort, which goes against the grain of human nature, it rubs your mind, will, and emotions wrong, and it totally causes your flesh to go into tilt mode. Because learning to use your faith is not easy, the weak, carnally minded, so-called Christians will make fun of and say dumb things about people who really are using faith to accomplish things. Those who really are fighting to please their heavenly Father, just like the elders of old, whom it is written about in Hebrews 11 as stated over and over, by faith…

Each and every one of these testimonies in Hebrews 11 noted a lot of spiritual effort involved. They had to override their mind, will, and emotions. It took a lot of action on their part, and I would be willing to bet that if you had the chance to ask any of them, they would say it was a lot of work bringing things to pass by faith. But it was well worth the effort, especially the completion of bringing something to pass by faith, which pleases God.

> *But without faith it is impossible to please him: for he that cometh to God must believe that he is, and that he is a rewarder of them that diligently seek him.* (Hebrews 11:6)

I've said it before, and I'll say it again: just because you know you are a possessor of faith (you have knowledge of God's word or know some of the Scriptures) does not mean you are pleasing God. You must be someone who is willing to use your faith to please God.

Because you possess faith, you now have the possibility of pleasing Him. Unless you're willing to use your faith, then you have not stepped over into the realm of doing things on purpose to please God.

FAITH GETS TO WORK

> *What doth it profit, my brethren, though a man say he hath faith, and have not works? can faith save him? If a brother or sister be naked, and destitute of daily food, and one of you say unto them (faith speaks), Depart in peace, be ye warmed and filled; notwithstanding ye give them not those things which are needful to the body; what doth it profit? Even so faith, if it hath not works, is dead, being alone.* (James 2:14–17)

James is the half-brother of Jesus, and if there was anyone who ever knew something about faith, it would be James. He saw Jesus use faith His whole life, making sure He was pleasing His heavenly Father.

Remember Romans 10:17, "So then faith comes by hearing, and hearing by the word of God." That's why Jesus spent so much time learning, knowing, and putting into practice the Scriptures. And, if you remember, Luke 4:16 says that it was His custom to go into the synagogue. But also in Luke 4:17, we see Jesus knew the Scriptures so well that He knew which book contained what Scripture and where to find Scriptures in that book. He could teach a message from the Scriptures.

> *And he came to Nazareth, where he had been brought up: and, as his custom was, he went into the synagogue on the sabbath day, and stood up for to read. And there was delivered unto him the book of the prophet Esaias. And when he had opened the book, he found the place where it was written.* (Luke 4:16–17)

It took a lot of work on Jesus's part to learn the Bible well enough to be able to do that. What about you? Is it your custom to attend church? Can you find the place in the Bible where it is written? Note: both of those are work!

So James saw Jesus release the power of faith with His words and also follow through with His actions over and over throughout his life, growing up with Jesus, right there in his home. Jesus's mother, Mary, knew this also. That is why at the wedding of Cana, Mary told the servants, "Do whatever He says to do." From that unique point of view, the book of James was written.

And James chapter 2:14 says (in my words),

> Does it do any good for you to say you have faith or speak words of faith and not follow up with corresponding actions? Without corresponding actions, can your release of faith do what you have desired it to do for you?

Then he gives a great example. James says, if you find a brother or sister who needs clothing or who needs food and one of you releases your faith with your words by saying unto the person needing clothing or the person needing food, "You be warmed and filled," that is a perfect picture of how to release faith; faith speaks. Faith is released by speaking words.

Then James goes on to say, "Notwithstanding, if you do not give them those things which are needful for them, whether it's clothing or whether it's food (that is works), did your words only help them in any way?"

There are times when the way you can release your faith is with your words only, in certain ministry times, or for things in your personal life. Generally speaking, actions are always required.

I like how John puts it in 1 John 3:17–18.

> *But whoso hath this world's good, and seeth his brother have need, and shutteth up his bowels of compassion from him, how dwelleth the love of God in him? My little children, let us not love in word, neither in tongue; but in deed and in truth.*

Yes, we release our faith with words, but we also follow through with works, or corresponding actions—deed and truth. Both James and John are saying the same thing. James goes on to say,

> *Even so faith, if it has not works, is dead, being alone.* (James 3:17)

James goes on to speak of how much work is actually involved sometimes in the natural realm once we have released our faith with our words for a desired result.

It is important to remember that faith is an unseen spiritual power that God, the Father, has made available for us to use to change things in the natural realm. We are using a principle that governs the operation of the unseen realm of heaven to effect change in the seen realm—the natural earthly realm or physical realm. Also we are using the unseen power of faith to override the systems that Satan has set up to keep us from fulfilling God's will for us in the earth. For either one of those to take place, it takes the use of words, and it takes a lot of work or effort to stay within the confines of the operation of heavenly principles.

James gives another example,

> *Was not Abraham our father justified by works, when he had offered Isaac his son upon the altar? Seest thou how faith wrought with his works, and by works was faith made perfect? And the scripture was fulfilled which saith, Abraham believed God, and it was imputed unto him for righteousness: and he was called the Friend of God. Ye see then how that by works a man is justified, and not by faith only.* (James 2:21–24)

I don't know if you have ever brought anything to pass by faith; I have many times. I can tell you this: it takes knowing God's word, the Bible. It takes believing God's word. It takes acting on God's word and then consistently acting as if God's word has already come to pass. From your natural thinking standpoint, it is not very easy to do, but it is doable.

It takes diligence, and it takes guarding your words so that you don't speak out of line with the word of God. It takes quoting scriptures over and over to keep your faith at a proper level for success. It takes no compromise but believing only. You must hold fast, and when doubt comes, you must let it pass through your mind and not stay. You must believe in your heart that those things that you have said will come to pass, so stick with that and act accordingly; it doesn't matter what anybody else says.

> *For what if some did not believe? Shall their unbelief make the faith of God without effect?* (Romans 3:3)

No, that's what Abraham had to do, and at first, he really didn't do a good job at it. God asked him (Abram) to leave his family, but he didn't. He brought his father with him, and he brought his nephew with him. Both became problems for him. He got stuck in the city of Haran for years until the death of his father. It was a big delay in the plan of God for his life. During that time, he acquired more employees and more responsibility, along with the responsibility of taking care of and training his nephew. He also had to deal with his own wife's carnal thinking. Not until he finally separated himself from his nephew did the fullness of God's plan start to work. Again, the Lord spoke to Abram, and when He did, faith was redeposited into Abram—God's faith—so it could be used to bring God's plan to pass for mankind through Abram.

> *And the Lord said unto Abram, after that Lot was separated from him, Lift up now thine eyes, and look from the place where thou art northward, and southward, and eastward, and westward: for all the land which thou seest, to thee will I give it, and to thy seed for ever. And I will make thy seed as the dust of the earth: so that if a man can number the dust of the earth, then shall thy seed also be numbered. Arise, walk through the land in the length of it and in the breadth of it; for I will give it unto thee.* (Genesis 13:14–17)

Once he left his nephew Lot, the Lord spoke to him again and changed his name to Abraham. Within a year, he and Sarah gave birth to the promised child, Issac.

> *And when Abram was ninety years old and nine, the Lord appeared to Abram, and said unto him, I am the Almighty God; walk before me, and be thou perfect. Neither shall thy name any more be called Abram, but thy name shall be Abraham; for a father of many nations have I made thee.* (Genesis 17:1, 5)

> *And the Lord visited Sarah as he had said, and the Lord did unto Sarah as he had spoken. For Sarah conceived, and bare Abraham a son in his old*

*age, at the set time of which God had spoken to him.
And Abraham was an hundred years old, when his
son Isaac was born unto him.* (Genesis 21:1, 2, 5)

From the first time the Lord spoke to Abram (*Stephen sheds light on this in Acts 7:2*). Until the time the Lord changed Abram's name to Abraham, Abraham's partial obedience caused him a lot of work and trouble along with no fulfillment of the promise "I will make of thee a great nation" (Genesis 12:2). But the moment Abraham started completely being obedient and saying what the Lord said (releasing faith), within a year, Isaac was born.

Abram had unbelief, not nonbelief. Nonbelief is not knowing any of the Bible. Even if a person has heard some Scripture, there is a refusal to believe it in any way. Nonbelief is a result of a hardened heart. Unbelief is knowing what the Lord has said, you say that you believe it, but choose to act and talk differently than what the word of God says. Unbelief is a result of doubt.

Romans 4 speaks very highly of Abraham's use of faith and doesn't even mention any of his mistakes. It also speaks that Abraham did not have righteousness imputed to him because of his works, doing things to make him look good in the Lord's sight. No, he had righteousness imputed to him because he believed what the Lord said, and at least he was trying to act on it, but he was influenced by his own reasoning.

What if Abram had been completely obedient and did not bring his father with him, did not bring Lot with him, but did exactly what the Lord had told him to do and leave his country and his people? Abram would not have had to linger in Haran for years, and then quite possibly, the famine may not have even come or may not have affected him. If he had been in complete obedience, then all the consequences that happened to his nephew Lot because of Abram bringing him may have been avoided.

I think Abram was reasoning within himself that his father was getting old, he needed to take care of him, and that Lot had lost his father, so he needed to be a father to Lot; for these reasons, he only partially obeyed the Lord's request of him. Even though Abram partially obeyed the Lord, it looks as though the Lord was pleased that he was at least trying to act on his word; by doing that, he was at least using faith.

When I say, "Faith gets to work" or "Faith works," I'm not saying faith is doing something to make a person righteous in God's sight. No, what I mean is, when you hear God's word and believe God's word, you start acting on it. It is spiritual work, sort of like when you know your job and do your job in the physical realm; that is called physical work.

We can see how hard it was on Abram to completely follow through on what the Lord had requested of him. It took him twenty-five years of battling back and forth with his own reasoning, with complete obedience, until the Lord finally stepped in and changed his name and gave him the choice to call himself what the Lord called him, the father of many nations.

If you will notice, the moment Abraham completely sold out and agreed with the Lord that he was the father of many nations, his wife Sarah became pregnant. I wonder how many years we have partially obeyed the Lord and missed out on what he was trying to accomplish in our lives.

One thing I've noticed in my personal life is that when I have made the rock-solid choice to stick with the promise made to me in the word of God, it has been very hard work keeping myself in line with that promise, not yielding to my own understanding, but holding fast to my confession of faith and to my actions in life as if the promise were already so.

Paul reveals he also found this out the hard way!

> *What shall we say then that Abraham our father, as pertaining to the flesh, hath found?* (Romans 4:1)

When we look at the life of Abraham, it shows us a picture: no matter how you receive a word from the Lord—whether you receive it from the Scriptures, or you receive it from God Himself appearing to you and speaking to you, as He did with Abraham—no matter how spectacular a way you receive a word from the Lord, you are still going to have to work hard to overcome your flesh, your reasoning, and the devil for the faith you received when you heard God's word to produce results.

Also, we see that you can make mistake after mistake, but as long as you hold on to the word of God, as long as you keep believing—even though at times you lean on your own understanding—the word of the Lord is still working to produce the desired result. We can see that Abraham found the more that you lean on your own understanding, the more you reason with yourself about what you think you should do instead of what the Lord told you to do, the longer it will take for your faith to produce the desired result.

Abraham received his first word from the Lord when he was seventy-five years old, and for twenty-four years, he partially obeyed God by leaning on his own understanding. Then in the twenty-fourth year, he finally separated himself from all his family. Now it was Abraham, his wife Sarah, and the Lord only, and in one year, his son, Isaac, was born unto him when Abraham was one hundred years old.

> *Trust in the Lord with all thine heart; and lean not unto thine own understanding. In all thy ways acknowledge him, and he shall direct thy paths.* (Proverbs 3:5–6)

Sometimes, if not most of the time, or even all the time, when using your faith to accomplish something, it is very hard work, not physical work but spiritual and mental work.

Accomplishing things by faith takes determination and the ability to stick to it. That is what the Bible calls patience. I'll give you a Scripture for it.

> *Cast not away therefore your confidence, which hath great recompence of reward. For ye have need of patience, that, after ye have done the will of God, ye might receive the promise. For yet a little*

while, and he that shall come will come, and will not tarry. Now the just shall live by faith: but if any man draw back, my soul shall have no pleasure in him. But we are not of them who draw back unto perdition; but of them that believe to the saving of the soul. (Hebrews 10:35–39)

Paul found out that when Abraham yielded to his natural thinking or to the fleshly way of thinking or living and did not stick to the words which the Lord had spoken to him, it caused Abraham a lot of wasted time and a lot of problems.

How do we know that Paul found this out? Because Paul leaned to his own understanding. Paul went the natural way of thinking, the way his flesh would desire, his personal reasoning of "This must be how it will work." Because of being misled, Paul did not stick to what Jesus told him on the road to Damascus, that he would go to the Gentiles first, the kings second, and then to the Jews third. Paul yielded to his natural desires and his natural fleshly way of thinking, which caused him many problems and a lot of wasted time. Let's look at it.

And there was a certain disciple at Damascus, named Ananias; and to him said the Lord in a vision, Ananias. And he said, Behold, I am here, Lord. And the Lord said unto him, Arise, and go into the street which is called Straight, and enquire in the house of Judas for one called Saul, of Tarsus: for, behold, he prayeth, and hath seen in a vision a man named Ananias coming in, and putting his hand on him, that he might receive his sight. Then Ananias answered, Lord, I have heard by many of this man, how much evil he hath done to thy saints at Jerusalem: and here he hath authority from the chief priests to bind all that call on thy name. But the Lord said unto him, Go thy way: for he is a chosen vessel unto me, to bear my name <u>before the</u>

Gentiles, and kings, and the children of Israel: for I will shew him how great things he must suffer for my name's sake. (Acts 9:10–16)

Jesus assigned Paul three specific duties.

1. Go to the Gentiles.
2. Witness before the kings.
3. Witness to the children of Israel.

This is Paul's personal testimony of the second time Jesus told Paul of his Gentile calling.

> *And it came to pass, that, when I was come again to Jerusalem, even while I prayed in the temple, I was in a trance; and saw him saying unto me, Make haste, and get thee quickly out of Jerusalem: for they will not receive thy testimony concerning me. And he said unto me, "Depart: for I will send thee far hence unto the Gentiles."* (Acts 22:17–18, 21)

Here is Paul's personal testimony of the first time Jesus gave him his assignment.

> *And I said, Who art thou, Lord? And he said, I am Jesus whom thou persecutest. But rise, and stand upon thy feet: for I have appeared unto thee for this purpose, to make thee a minister and a witness both of these things which thou hast seen, and of those things in the which I will appear unto thee; delivering thee from the people, and from the Gentiles, unto whom now I send thee, to open their eyes, and to turn them from darkness to light, and from the power of Satan unto God, that they may receive forgiveness of sins, and inheritance among*

them which are sanctified by faith that is in me.
(Acts 26:15–18)

At least twice, Jesus personally told Paul that He had sent him to the Gentiles and not to his own nationality, the Jewish people. But Paul kept going to the Jewish people first, which caused him much suffering and much delay in the advancing of the kingdom of heaven.

Let's look at a few scriptures, showing us this.

And straightway he preached Christ in the synagogues, that he is the Son of God. But all that heard him were amazed, and said; Is not this he that destroyed them which called on this name in Jerusalem, and came hither for that intent, that he might bring them bound unto the chief priests? But Saul increased the more in strength, and confounded the Jews which dwelt at Damascus, proving that this is very Christ. And after that many days were fulfilled, the Jews took counsel to kill him. (Acts 9:20–23)

And when they were at Salamis, they preached the word of God in the synagogues of the Jews: and they had also John to their minister. (Acts 13:5)

And when the Jews were gone out of the synagogue, the Gentiles besought that these words might be preached to them the next sabbath. (Acts 13:42)

The Gentiles received the gospel. The Jews rejected the gospel and Paul.

But when the Jews saw the multitudes, they were filled with envy, and spake against those things

> *which were spoken by Paul, contradicting and blaspheming.*
>
> *But the Jews stirred up the devout and honourable women, and the chief men of the city, and raised persecution against Paul and Barnabas, and expelled them out of their coasts. (Acts 13:45–50)*

> *And it came to pass in Iconium, that they went both together into the synagogue of the Jews, and so spake, that a great multitude both of the Jews and also of the Greeks believed. But the unbelieving Jews stirred up the Gentiles, and made their minds evil affected against the brethren. And there came thither certain Jews from Antioch and Iconium, who persuaded the people, and, having stoned Paul, drew him out of the city, supposing he had been dead. (Acts 14:1, 2, 19)*

The Jews persecuted Paul.

> *And when they were come, and had gathered the church together, they rehearsed all that God had done with them, and how he had opened the door of faith unto the Gentiles. (Acts 14:27)*

Paul finally had all the partial obedience he could stand and all the beating and rejection he could take from the Jews. He accepted his assignment from Jesus and declared, "I am going to the Gentiles!"

> *And he reasoned in the synagogue every sabbath, and persuaded the Jews and the Greeks. And when Silas and Timotheus were come from Macedonia, Paul was pressed in the spirit, and testified to the Jews that Jesus was Christ. And when they opposed themselves, and blasphemed, he shook his raiment, and said unto them, Your blood be upon*

your own heads; I am clean: from henceforth I will go unto the Gentiles. And he departed thence, and entered into a certain man's house, named Justus, one that worshipped God, whose house joined hard to the synagogue. And Crispus, the chief ruler of the synagogue, believed on the Lord with all his house; and many of the Corinthians hearing believed, and were baptized. (Acts 18:4–8)

The Corinthians were the wildest, lowdown, drunkest bunch of Gentiles you could find, yet unlike the Jews, they received Paul and the gospel. Paul even reminded them of this.

Know ye not that the unrighteous shall not inherit the kingdom of God? Be not deceived: neither fornicators, nor idolaters, nor adulterers, nor effeminate, nor abusers of themselves with mankind, nor thieves, nor covetous, nor drunkards, nor revilers, nor extortioners, shall inherit the kingdom of God. And such were some of you;
but ye are washed, but ye are sanctified, but ye are justified in the name of the Lord Jesus, and by the Spirit of our God. (1 Corinthians 6:9–11)

This one uncompromising act of obedience (leave the Jews alone) instantly caused Paul's ministry to flourish, just like Abraham's one act of uncompromising obedience (leave your family) caused his life to flourish.

Something we must notice here: it was very hard work for Paul to turn from the Jews and go after the Gentiles first. It took all the faith he had. Paul was taught from a young age that Gentiles were the lowest form of people and that he should not even associate with them or speak with them. He had to overcome many traditional obstacles in his life to turn his attention to fulfilling Jesus's purpose for his life. It was a lot of hard work to go against everything he was taught. That's probably why he kept going to the Jews first. To Paul, it seemed the most natural, most compassionate thing he could do was to reach out to his own people, the Jews.

He probably reasoned to himself that they knew who he was, they knew what he had done, and if they saw him as a changed man, surely, they would receive Jesus and the message of salvation through him. But they didn't; they rejected him and beat him, whipped him, and stoned him. Why? Because Jesus assigned Paul to the Gentiles and Peter to the Jews.

The most natural thing to Paul (ministering to the Jews) turned out to be the hardest thing he had ever done. The most unnatural thing (ministering to the Gentiles) turned out to be the easiest and most beneficial thing Paul had ever done.

Paul continually reminds us through his writings that fulfilling Jesus's purpose for our lives, which is living by faith, can be hard work.

It was not natural for Paul to go to the Gentiles.

It was not natural for Noah to build a boat when it had never even rained.

It was not natural for Abraham and Sarah to give birth to a child being nearly a hundred years old.

It was not natural for Moses to say each of the plagues was going to happen, nor was it natural for the Red Sea to split by just stretching out a rod toward it, nor for manna to appear daily, or for water to come from a rock, and all the other things that happened by faith to the children of Israel.

It was not natural for the Jordan River to dry up so Joshua and the children of Israel could cross it.

It was not natural for the walls of Jericho to fall just by a shout.

It was not natural for Gideon to defeat such a huge army with so few men.

You can go to Hebrews 11 and go through every one of the examples given about what was accomplished by faith, and none of them were natural.

I'm saying this because, when you and I do things by faith, it is not going to be natural nor will it be a normal thing for us to do.

It is not natural to speak to your mountain and tell it to move.

It is not natural for you to pray and believe you receive when you pray.

It is not natural for you to lay hands on sick people, and Jesus's power works through you and heals them.

It is not natural for you to tithe.

It is not natural for you to give, and then it be given to you.

It is not natural to forgive those who have harmed you.

Pretty much everything we do by faith has been designed by God to not be natural for us to do.

If there is one statement that could be made which would relate to what it is like to do things by faith, it would be to do things by faith is work.

Paul said, "We are laborers together with God."

Look at this Scripture and notice how many times Paul says "being a builder or work."

> *According to the grace of God which is given unto me, as a wise masterbuilder, I have laid the foundation, and another buildeth thereon. But let every man take heed how he buildeth thereupon. For other foundation can no man lay than that is laid, which is Jesus Christ. Now if any man build upon this foundation gold, silver, precious stones, wood, hay, stubble; every man's work shall be made manifest: for the day shall declare it, because it shall be revealed by fire; and the fire shall try every man's work of what sort it is. If any man's work abide which he hath built thereupon, he shall receive a reward. If any man's work shall be burned, he shall suffer loss: but he himself shall be saved; yet so as by fire.* (1 Corinthians 3:10–15)

Just think how much work is involved on the Holy Spirit's part to get us to do anything. We are all called to preach the gospel to every creature. Preaching the gospel takes effort; it takes work. To know what and how to preach takes studying (I'm not even talking about behind a podium). To study is work. Prayer is work. Walking in love is work. Being a faithful member of Jesus's church is work. Being on time and finding your place in the work that it takes to make the organization of the church operate involves work. If you and I will notice, everything in God's kingdom is designed for diligent people, not for lazy people. Anybody can be scared, lazy, late, and unfaithful.

This is some of what Jesus has to say about you and me being faithful to His work.

> *His lord said unto him, Well done, thou good and faithful servant: thou hast been faithful over a few things, I will make thee ruler over many things: enter thou into the joy of thy lord.* (Matthew 25:21)

Peter put it this way.

> *And beside this, giving all diligence... Wherefore the rather, brethren, give diligence to make your calling and election sure: for if ye do these things, ye shall never fall.* (2 Peter 1:5, 10)

Everything you do involves your release of faith along with corresponding actions (work) to fulfill any purpose. James's teaching on faith just straight out says it is work.

> *But whoso looketh into the perfect law of liberty, and continueth therein, he being not a forgetful hearer, but a doer of the work, this man shall be blessed in his deed.* (James 1:25)

James is teaching the pattern: hear the word, believe the word, then act on the word. Then, in chapter 2, he goes on to give examples of Abraham doing exactly this and says that what Abraham was involved in was work. Don't just think about physical labor; this is spiritual labor and mental labor, which is what it takes to accomplish things by faith.

It takes the force of patience to help our faith succeed. Patience is the ability to stick to it. Never give up, never give in, no matter how hard, no matter how long it may take, and no matter how heavy the load may feel. Patience helps us bear the load and the pressure of the test that our faith goes through while it is striving to produce the results we desire.

> *Knowing this, that the trying of your faith worketh patience. But let patience have her perfect work, that ye may be perfect and entire, wanting nothing.* (James 1:3, 4)

This is how the *Message* version states James 1:3–4:

> *Consider it a sheer gift, friends, when tests and challenges come at you from all sides. You know that under pressure, your faith-life is forced into the open and shows its true colors. So don't try to get out of anything prematurely. Let it do its work so you become mature and well-developed, not deficient in any way.*

The sooner you start practicing using your faith, which you obtained through your knowledge of God's word, the sooner you'll start seeing results.

> *But without faith it is impossible to please him: for he that cometh to God must believe that he is, and that he is a rewarder of them that diligently seek him.* (Hebrews 11:6)

Do you have a better understanding of what God kind of faith is? Do you understand the value that God Himself puts on faith and the seriousness He expects us to have concerning all aspects of faith?

He is the one himself who said, "Without faith, it is impossible to please Him!"

Should we consider faith as just some religious term or should we consider it to be way more than that?

Can you name the four characteristics of faith?

How is faith obtained?

Can faith become yours and can faith be developed?

Paul in Ephesians 6 called faith a shield. Sometimes, when you're standing, confessing the Scriptures, believing for them to come to pass while Satan is shooting fiery dart after fiery dart, and you look over at the front of your shield, and there are all these fiery darts stuck in there, and your shield is glowing red, you just hold on because your faith will eventually quench all of them, and Satan will run out of effort and fiery darts to attack you with, and you will be victorious.

> *Only be thou strong and very courageous, that thou mayest observe to do according to all the law, which Moses my servant commanded thee: turn not from it to the right hand or to the left, that thou mayest prosper whithersoever thou goest. This book of the law shall not depart out of thy mouth; but thou shalt meditate therein day and night, that thou mayest observe to do according to all that is written therein: for then thou shalt make thy way prosperous, and then thou shalt have good success. Have not I commanded thee? Be strong and of a good courage; be not afraid, neither be thou dismayed: for the Lord thy God is with thee whithersoever thou goest.* (Joshua 1:7–9)

I will end with this—God's personal testimony of what can be accomplished using faith:

> *The fundamental fact of existence is that this trust in God, this faith, is the firm foundation under*

everything that makes life worth living. It's our handle on what we can't see. The act of faith is what distinguished our ancestors, set them above the crowd. By faith, we see the world called into existence by God's word, what we see created by what we don't see. By an act of faith, Abel brought a better sacrifice to God than Cain. It was what he believed, not what he brought, that made the difference. That's what God noticed and approved as righteous. After all these centuries, that belief continues to catch our notice. By an act of faith, Enoch skipped death completely. "They looked all over and couldn't find him because God had taken him." We know on the basis of reliable testimony that before he was taken "he pleased God." It's impossible to please God apart from faith. And why? Because anyone who wants to approach God must believe both that he exists and that he cares enough to respond to those who seek him. By faith, Noah built a ship in the middle of dry land. He was warned about something he couldn't see, and acted on what he was told. The result? His family was saved. His act of faith drew a sharp line between the evil of the unbelieving world and the rightness of the believing world. As a result, Noah became intimate with God. By an act of faith, Abraham said yes to God's call to travel to an unknown place that would become his home. When he left he had no idea where he was going. By an act of faith he lived in the country promised him, lived as a stranger camping in tents. Isaac and Jacob did the same, living under the same promise. Abraham did it by keeping his eye on an unseen city with real, eternal foundations—the City designed and built by God. By faith, barren Sarah was able to become pregnant, old woman as she was at the time, because she believed the One who made a promise would do what he said. That's how it happened that from one man's dead and shriveled loins there are now people numbering into the millions.

* * *

Each one of these people of faith died not yet having in hand what was promised, but still believing. How did they do it? They saw it way off in the distance, waved their greeting, and accepted the fact that they were transients in this world. People who live this way make it plain that they are looking for their true home. If they were homesick for the old country, they could have gone back any time they wanted. But they were after a far better country than that—heaven country. You can see why God is so proud of them, and has a City waiting for them. By faith, Abraham, at the time of testing, offered Isaac back to God. Acting in faith, he was as ready to return the promised son, his only son, as he had been to receive him—and this after he had already been told, "Your descendants shall come from Isaac." Abraham figured that if God wanted to, he could raise the dead. In a sense, that's what happened when he received Isaac back, alive from off the altar. By an act of faith, Isaac reached into the future as he blessed Jacob and Esau. By an act of faith, Jacob on his deathbed blessed each of Joseph's sons in turn, blessing them with God's blessing, not his own—as he bowed worshipfully upon his staff. By an act of faith, Joseph, while dying, prophesied the exodus of Israel, and made arrangements for his own burial. By an act of faith, Moses' parents hid him away for three months after his birth. They saw the child's beauty, and they braved the king's decree. By faith, Moses, when grown, refused the privileges of the Egyptian royal house. He chose a hard life with God's people rather than an opportunistic soft life of sin with the oppressors. He valued suffering in the Messiah's camp far greater than Egyptian wealth because he was looking ahead, anticipating the pay-off. By an act of faith, he turned his heel on Egypt, indifferent to the king's blind rage. He had his eye on the One no eye can see, and kept right on going. By an act of faith, he kept the Passover Feast and sprinkled Passover blood on each house so that the destroyer of the firstborn wouldn't touch them. By an act of faith, Israel walked through the Red Sea on dry ground. The Egyptians tried it and drowned. By faith, the Israelites marched around the walls of Jericho for seven days, and the walls fell flat. By an act of faith, Rahab, the Jericho harlot, welcomed the spies and escaped the destruction that came on those who refused to trust God.

* * *

I could go on and on, but I've run out of time. There are so many more—Gideon, Barak, Samson, Jephthah, David, Samuel, the prophets. Through acts of faith, they toppled kingdoms, made justice work, took the promises for themselves. They were protected from lions, fires, and sword thrusts, turned disadvantage to advantage, won battles, routed alien armies. Women received their loved ones back from the dead. There were those who, under torture, refused to give in and go free, preferring something better: resurrection. Others braved abuse and whips, and, yes, chains and dungeons. We have stories of those who were stoned, sawed in two, murdered in cold blood; stories of vagrants wandering the earth in animal skins, homeless, friendless, powerless—the world didn't deserve them!—making their way as best they could on the cruel edges of the world. Not one of these people, even though their lives of faith were exemplary, got their hands on what was promised. God had a better plan for us: that their faith and our faith would come together to make one completed whole, their lives of faith not complete apart from ours. Do you see what this means—all these pioneers who blazed the way, all these veterans cheering us on? It means we'd better get on with it. Strip down, start running—and never quit! No extra spiritual fat, no parasitic sins. Keep your eyes on Jesus, who both began and finished this race we're in. Study how he did it. Because he never lost sight of where he was headed—that exhilarating finish in and with God—he could put up with anything along the way: Cross, shame, whatever. And now he's there, in the place of honor, right alongside God. When you find yourselves flagging in your faith, go over that story again, item by item, that long litany of hostility he plowed through. That will shoot adrenaline into your souls! (Hebrews 11:1–12:3 MSG)

Thank You, Jesus.

Faith is not merely a religious term.

Faith is a power that God has made available for us to learn how to develop and use.

Faith is a law that you have the right to set in motion and keep in full force.

Faith is a substance for you to apply to mountains to move them out of your life or apply to things you need or desire to bring them into your life.

Faith is a servant, on duty for you to benefit from, to aid and assist you as you fulfill the Lord's will for your life, so at the end of your life you will hear, "Well done," but not until you have done all that was required of you with the assistance of your servant, faith.

Faith comes and is deposited within your spirit each and every time you hear the word of God. That is why you must guard and protect your spirit at all costs.

> *Keep thy heart with all diligence; for out of it*
> *are the issues of life.* (Proverbs 4:22)

Faith is released, activated, or applied by speaking God's word. Speak to the problems the devil is using to block your access to fulfilling God's will for your life. Faith sees the desired result way before the natural realm reveals any changes. Faith stands, never gives up, holds on to the promise, holds out, is never moved off its desire, and never gives in. Under great pressure, faith is not crushed; it may be bent but not broken and withstands all, and having done all to stand, faith stands. Faith praises, thanks, and worships always in all situations, never blames God, gives honor and glory to God always, and stays in peace.

If we keep our faith in full force and our praise continually empowering our faith, sickness will not be successful in its attack against our body. Poverty will not be able to stay and dominate your life. Your children will make heaven. Your marriage will be blessed. Your understanding of the Lord's will for your life will be known by you; you will bear much fruit in your life and be a blessing to the kingdom of heaven. Faith—God's faith—is one of the keys to the kingdom of heaven for our success (John 3:18).

ABOUT THE AUTHOR

Paul Peresich is the founder and senior minister of the Mission Church and Training Center in Saucier, Mississippi. His vision is to win the lost and teach the saved and to see every member of the body of Christ filled with the knowledge of God's will and plan for their life, fulfilling this plan in a lifestyle worthy of the Lord Jesus. Paul has been serving Jesus since 1982, teaching biblical principles in a clear, easily understandable, and doable manner. He was ordained in India under Apostle Gaddam Thomas and also under Bishop Bill Hamon, Christian International, Santa Rosa, Beach Florida.